Streetez...

Aberaeron	27
Aberporth	35
Aberystwyth	7
Ammanford	9
Brynamman	27
Cardigan	19
Carmarthen	11
Cross Hands	20
Drefach	28
Ferryside	35
Fishguard & Goodwick	21
Glanaman & Garnant	22
Haverfordwest	13
Kilgetty	36
Lampeter	28
Laugharne	36
Llandeilo	29
Llandovery	29
Llandybie	30
Llandysul	37
...ord Haven	15
Narberth	30
Newcastle Emlyn	31
Newport	31
New Quay	32
Neyland	32
Pembroke	23
Pembroke Dock	17
Pen-y-Groes & Saron	25
Pontyberem	24
St. Clears	33
St. David's	33
St. Florence	37
Saundersfoot	34
Tenby	26
Tregaron	37
Tumble	34
Whitland	35

Key to street plans
Allwedd i blaniau stryd

Plans drawn at a scale of 4 inches to 1 mile
Aruluniwyd y planiau yn ôl y raddfa 4 modfedd i 1 filltir

Symbol	English	Welsh
M4	Motorway	Traffordd
A48	A road (Trunk road)	Ffordd A (Priffordd)
A48	Dual carriageway	Ffordd ddeuol
B4281	B road	Ffordd B
	Through road	Ffordd drwodd
- - - - -	Track/Footpath	Llwybr/Llwybr troed
-·-·-·-	County boundary	Ffin sirol
-··-··-	Municipal boundary	Ffin fwrdeisiol
▬▬	Railway	Rheilffordd
	Woods and forest	Coedtir a choedwig

Symbol	English	Welsh
P	Car parks (major)	(prif) Maes parcio
☾†✡	Places of worship	Mannau addoliad
🏨🍺	Hotel/Public house	Gwesty/Tafarndy
⛽	Petrol station	Gorsaf betrol
🔔	Police station	Gorsaf heddlu
✉	Post Office	Swyddfa'r Post
M 🎭	Theatre/Museum	Theatr/Amgueddfa
T	Toilet facility	Cyfleustra toiled
✚	Health centre	Canolfan iechyd
🚐	Caravan site	Safleoedd carafannau

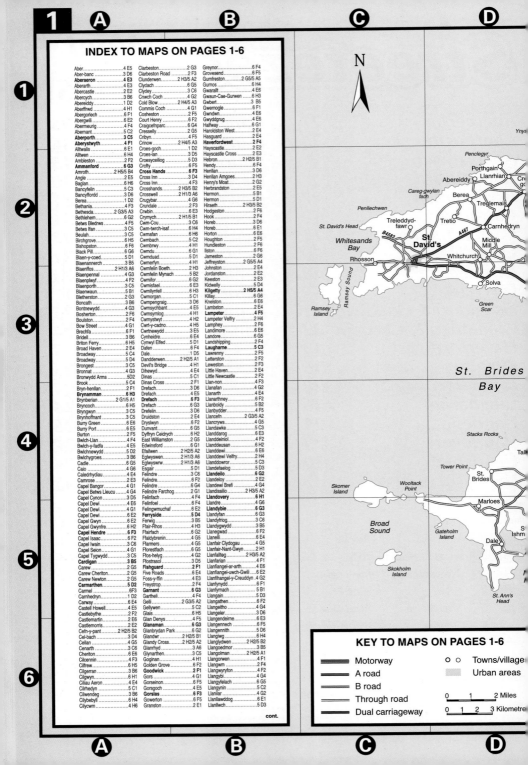

INDEX TO MAPS ON PAGES 1-6

Aber....4 E5
Aber-banc....3 D6
Aberaeron....4 E3
Aberarth....4 E3
Abercastle....2 E2
Abercych....3 B6
Abereiddy....1 D2
Aberffrwd....4 H1
Abergorlech....6 F1
Abergwili....6 E2
Abermeurig....4 F4
Abernant....5 C2
Aberporth....3 C5
Aberystwyth....4 F1
Alltwalis....6 E1
Alltwen....6 H4
Ambleston....2 F2
Ammanford....6 G3
Amroth....2 H5/5 B4
Angle....2 E5
Baglan....6 H6
Bancyfelin....5 C3
Bancyffordd....3 D6
Berea....1 D2
Bethania....4 F3
Bethesda....2 G3/5 A3
Bethlehem....6 G2
Betws Bledrws....4 F5
Betws Ifan....3 C5
Beulah....3 C5
Birchgrove....6 H5
Bishopston....6 F6
Black Pill....6 G6
Blaen-y-coed....5 D1
Blaenannerch....3 B5
Blaenffos....2 H1/3 A6
Blaenpennal....4 G3
Blaenplwyf....4 F2
Blaenporth....3 D5
Blaenwaun....5 B1
Bletherston....2 G3
Boncath....3 B6
Bontnewydd....4 G3
Bosherton....2 F6
Boulston....2 F4
Bow Street....4 G1
Brechfa....6 F1
Bridell....3 B6
Briton Ferry....6 H5
Broad Haven....2 E4
Broadway....5 C4
Broadway....5 D4
Brongest....3 C5
Bronnat....4 G3
Bronwydd Arms....5D2
Brook....5 C4
Bryn-henllan....2 F1
Brynamman....6 H3
Brynberian....2 G1/5 A1
Bryncoch....6 H5
Bryngwyn....3 C5
Brynhoffnant....3 C5
Burry Green....6 E6
Burry Port....6 E6
Burton....2 F5
Bwlch-Llan....4 F4
Bwlch-y-fadfa....4 E5
Bwlchnewydd....5 D2
Bwlchygroes....3 B6
Cadle....6 G5
Caio....6 G1
Caledrhydiau....4 E4
Camrose....2 E3
Capel Bangor....4 G1
Capel Betws Lleucu....4 G4
Capel Cynon....3 D5
Capel Dewi....4 E6
Capel Dewi....4 G1
Capel Dewi....6 E2
Capel Gwyn....6 E2
Capel Gwynfe....6 H2
Capel Hendre....6 F3
Capel Isaac....6 F2
Capel Iwan....3 C6
Capel Seion....4 G1
Capel Tygwydd....3 C5
Cardigan....3 B5
Carew....2 G5
Carew Cheriton....2 G5
Carew Newton....2 G5
Carmarthen....5 D2
Carmel....6F3
Carnhedryn....1 D2
Carway....6 E4
Castell Howell....4 E5
Castlebythe....2 F2
Castlemartin....2 E6
Castlemorris....2 E2
Cefn-y-pant....2 H2/5 B2
Cei-bach....3 D4
Cellan....4 G5
Cenarth....3 C6
Cheriton....6 E6
Cilcennin....4 F3
Cilfrew....6 H5
Cilgerran....3 B6
Cilgwyn....6 H1
Ciliau Aeron....4 E4
Cilrhedyn....5 C1
Cilwendeg....3 B6
Cilybebyll....6 H4
Cilycwm....4 H6

Clarbeston....2 G3
Clarbeston Road....2 F3
Clunderwen....2 H3/5 A2
Clydach....6 G5
Clydey....3 C6
Cnwch Coch....4 G2
Cold Blow....2 H4/5 A3
Commis Coch....4 G1
Cosheston....2 F5
Court Henry....6 F2
Craigcefnparc....6 G4
Cresselly....2 G5
Cribyn....4 F5
Crinow....2 H4/5 A3
Croes-goch....1 D2
Croes-lan....3 D5
Croesyceiliog....5 D3
Crofty....6 F5
Cross Hands....6 F3
Cross Inn....3 D4
Cross Inn....4 F3
Crosshands....2 H3/5 B2
Crosswell....2 H1/3 A6
Crugybar....4 G6
Crundale....2 F3
Crwbin....6 E4
Crymych....2 H1/5 B1
Cwm-Cou....3 C6
Cwm-twrch-isaf....6 H4
Cwmafan....6 H6
Cwmbach....5 C2
Cwmbrwy....4 H1
Cwmdu....6 G1
Cwmduad....5 D1
Cwmerfyn....4 H1
Cwmfelin Boeth....2 H3
Cwmfelin Mynach....5 B2
Cwmifor....6 G2
Cwmisfael....6 E3
Cwmllynfell....6 H3
Cwmorgan....5 C1
Cwmpengraig....3 D6
Cwmsychbant....4 E5
Cwmsymlog....4 H1
Cwmystwyt....4 H2
Cwrt-y-cadno....4 H5
Cwrtnewydd....3 E5
Cynheidre....6 E4
Cynwyl Elfed....5 D1
Dafen....6 F4
Dale....1 D5
Dandderwen....2 H2/5 A1
Devil's Bridge....4 H1
Dihewyd....4 E4
Dinas....5 C1
Dinas Cross....2 F1
Drefach....3 D6
Drefach....4 E5
Drefach....6 F3
Drefach....6 G3
Drefelin....3 D6
Druidston....2 E4
Dryslwyn....6 F2
Dunvant....6 G5
Dyffryn Ceidrych....6 H2
East Williamston....2 G5
Edwinsford....6 G1
Efailwen....2 H2/5 A2
Eglwyswen....2 H1/3 A6
Eglwyswrw....2 H1/3 A6
Espair....5 D1
Felindre....3 C6
Felindre....6 F2
Felindre....6 G4
Felindre Farchog....2 G1
Felinfach....4 F4
Felinfoel....6 F4
Felingwmuchaf....6 E2
Ferryside....5 D4
Ferwig....3 B5
Ffair-Rhos....4 H3
Ffairfach....6 G2
Ffaldybrenin....4 G5
Ffarmers....4 G5
Fforestfach....6 G5
Ffos-helyg....4 G2
Ffostrasol....3 C5
Fishguard....2 F1
Five Roads....6 E4
Foss-y-ffin....4 E3
Freystrop....2 F4
Garnant....6 G3
Gartheli....4 F4
Gelli....2 G3/5 A2
Gellywen....5 C2
Glais....6 H5
Glan Denys....4 F5
Glanaman....6 G3
Glanbrydan Park....6 G2
Glandwr....2 H2/5 B1
Glandy Cross....2 H2/5 A2
Glanrhyd....3 A6
Glynarthen....3 C5
Goginan....4 H1
Golden Grove....6 F2
Goodwick....2 F1
Gors....4 G1
Gorseinon....6 F5
Gorsgoch....4 E5
Gorslas....6 F3
Gowerton....6 F5
Granston....2 E1

Greynor....6 F4
Grovesend....6 F5
Gumfreston....2 G5/5 A5
Gumos....6 H4
Gwarallt....4 E6
Gwaun-Cae-Gurwen....6 H3
Gwbert....3 B5
Gwernogle....6 F1
Gwndwn....4 E6
Gwyddgrug....4 E6
Halfway....6 G1
Haroldston West....2 E4
Hasguard....2 E4
Haverfordwest....2 F4
Hayscastle....2 E2
Hayscastle Cross....2 E3
Hebron....2 H2/5 B1
Hendy....6 F4
Henllan....1 D6
Henllan Amgoes....2 H3
Henry's Moat....2 G2
Herbrandston....2 E5
Hermon....5 B1
Hermon....5 D1
Hiraeth....2 H3/5 B2
Hodgeston....2 F6
Hook....2 F4
Horeb....3 D6
Horeb....6 E1
Horton....6 E6
Houghton....2 F5
Hundleston....2 F6
Ilston....6 F6
Jameston....2 G6
Jeffreyston....2 G5/5 A4
Johnston....2 E4
Jordanston....2 E2
Keeston....2 E3
Kidwelly....5 D4
Kilgetty....2 H5/5 A4
Killay....6 G6
Knelston....6 E6
Lampeter....2 E4
Lampeter....4 F5
Lampeter Velfry....2 H4
Lamphey....2 F6
Landimore....6 E6
Landore....6 G5
Landshipping....2 F4
Laugharne....5 C3
Lawrenny....2 F5
Letterston....2 F2
Lewestone....2 F3
Little Haven....2 E4
Little Newcastle....2 F2
Llan-non....4 F3
Llanafan....4 G2
Llanarth....4 E4
Llananthney....6 F2
Llanboidy....5 B2
Llanbydder....4 F5
Llancefn....2 G3/5 A2
Llancryws....4 G5
Llandawke....5 C3
Llandarog....6 E3
Llanddeiniol....4 F2
Llanddeusan....6 H2
Llanddewi....6 E6
Llanddewi Velfry....2 H4
Llanddowror....5 C3
Llandefaelog....5 D3
Llandeilo....6 G2
Llandeloy....2 E2
Llandewi Brefi....4 G4
Llandissilio....2 H3/5 A2
Llandovery....6 H1
Llandybie....6 G3
Llandyfan....6 G3
Llandyfriog....3 C6
Llandygwydd....3 B5
Llanegwad....6 F2
Llanelli....6 E4
Llanfair Clydogau....4 G5
Llanfair-Nant-Gwyn....2 H1
Llanfallteg....2 H3/5 A2
Llanfarian....4 F1
Llanfihangel-ar-arth....4 E6
Llanfihangel-uwch-Gwili....6 E2
Llanfihangel-y-Creuddyn....4 G2
Llanfynydd....6 F1
Llanfyrnach....5 B1
Llangain....5 D3
Llangathen....6 F2
Llangeitho....4 G4
Llangeler....3 D6
Llangendeirne....6 E3
Llangennech....6 F5
Llangennith....5 D6
Llangiwg....6 H4
Llanglydwen....2 H2/5 B2
Llangoedmor....3 B5
Llangolman....2 H2/5 A1
Llangower....4 F1
Llangwm....2 F4
Llangwyryfon....4 F2
Llangybi....4 G4
Llangyfelach....6 G5
Llangynin....5 C2
Llanilar....4 G2
Llanllawddog....6 E1
Llanllwch....5 D3

cont.

KEY TO MAPS ON PAGES 1-6

Motorway
A road
B road
Through road
Dual carriageway

o o Towns/village
Urban areas

0 1 2 Miles
0 1 2 3 Kilometre

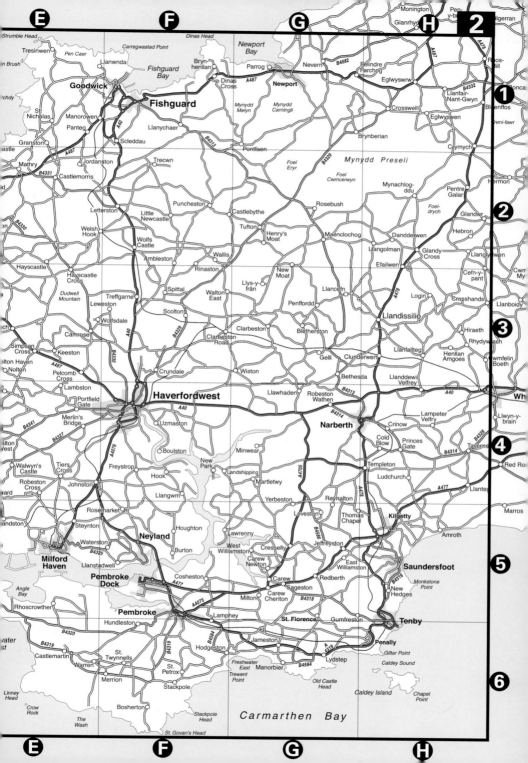

Llanilwni 4 E6
Llanmadoc 6 E6
Llanmiloe 5 C4
Llanmorlais 6 F5
Llannon 6 F4
Llanpumsaint 5 D1
Llanrhian 1 D2
Llanrhidian 6 E6
Llanrhystud 4 F2
Llansadurnen 5 C4
Llansaint 6 H5
Llansantffraed 4 E3
Llansawel 4 G6
Llanstadwell 2 F5
Llanstephan 5 D4
Llanteg 2 H4/5 B4
Llanwenog 4 E5
Llanwinio 5 C2
Llanwnda 2 E1
Llanwnnen 4 F5
Llanwrda 6 H1
Llanybri 5 C3
Llanychaer 2 F1
Llanynog 5 C3
Llawhaden 2 G4
Llechryd 3 B5
Lledrod 4 G2
Llidiad-Nenog 4 F6
Lliundain-fach 4 F4
Llwyn-y-brain 5 B3
Llwyn-y-groes 4 E4
Llwyncelyn 4 E4
Llwyndafydd 3 D4
Llys-y-frân 2 G3
Login 2 H3/5 A2
Loughor 6 F5
Loveston 2 G5/5 A4
Ludchurch 2 H4/5 A3
Lydstep 2 G6/5 B5
Maenclochog 2 G2/5 A1
Maescrugiau 4 E6
Maesllyn 3 D5
Maesybont 6 F3
Manorbier 2 G6
Manordeilo 6 G2
Manorowen 2 E1
Margam 6 H6
Marloes 1 D5
Marros 5 B4

Martletwy 2 G4
Mathry 2 E2
Meidrim 5 C2
Merlin's Bridge 2 F4
Merrion 2 F6
Merthyr 5 D2
Middle Mill 1 D2
Milford Haven 2 E5
Milton 2 G5
Minwear 2 G4
Monachty 4 E3
Monington 3 A5
Morfa Bach 5 D3
Morriston 6 G5
Moylgrove 3 A5
Myddfai 6 H1
Mydroilyn 4 E4
Mynachlog-ddu 2 H2/5 A1
Nanternis 3 D4
Nantgaredig 6 E2
Nantycaws 6 E3
Narberth 2 G4/5 A3
Neath 6 H5
Nebo 4 F3
Nevern 2 G1/3 A6
New Hedges 2 H5/5 A4
New Inn 4 E6
New Moat 2 G3
New Park 2 F4
New Quay 3 D4
Newcastle Emlyn 3 C6
Newchapel 2 G1
Newchurch 5 D2
Newgale 2 E3
Newport 2 G1
Newton 6 F6
Neyland 2 F5
Nicholaston 6 F6
Nolton 2 E3
Nolton Haven 2 E3
Oakford 4 E4
Oxwich 6 E6
Pant-lasau 6 G5
Panteg 2 E1
Pantglas Hall 6 F3
Pantgwyn 3 B5
Parc-Henri 6 E4
Parcllyn 3 B4
Parkmill 6 F6

Parrog 2 G1
Pelcomb Cross 2 E3
Pembrey 5 D5
Pembroke 2 F5
Pembroke Dock 2 F5
Pen-bont 4 G1
Pen-y-banc 6 G2
Pen-y-bont 5 C2
Pen-y-bryn 3 B6
Pen-y-garn 6 F1
Pen-y-groes 6 F3
Penally 2 H6/5 A5
Penant 4 E3
Penbryn 3 C4
Pencader 4 E6
Pencarreg 4 F5
Penclawdd 6 F5
Pendine 5 B4
Penffordd 2 G3
Penherder 3 C6
Penllergaer 6 G5
Penmaen 6 F6
Pennant 6 F6
Penparc 3 B5
Penparcau 4 F1
Penrhiw-llan 3 D5
Penrhiwpal 3 D5
Penrice 6 F2
Pentre Galar 2 H2/5 B1
Pentre-Gwenlais 6 G3
Pentre-bâch 4 F5
Pentre-cwrt 3 D6
Pentre-llyn 4 G2
Pentrebach 6 F4
Pentrecagal 3 C6
Pentrefelin 6 F2
Pentregat 3 D5
Penuwch 4 F3
Penycwm 2 E3
Plwmp 3 D4
Pont Creuddyn 4 F4
Pont Henry 6 E3
Pont Silin 4 E5
Pont-rhyd-y-groes 4 H2
Pontamman 6 G3

Ponterwyd 4 H1
Pontfaen 2 G1
Pontgarreg 3 D4
Ponthirwaun 3 C5
Pontlliw 6 G5
Pontrhydfendigaid 4 H3
Pontrhydyfen 6 H5
Pontyates 5 E4
Pontyberem 6 E3
Port Eynon 6 E6
Port Talbot 6 H6
Portfield Gate 2 E4
Porthgain 1 D2
Porthyrhyd 6 F3
Princes Gate 2 H4/5 A3
Pumpsaint 4 G6
Puncheston 2 F2
Pwll 6 E5
Pwll-trap 5 C3
Red Roses 5 B3
Redberth 2 G5/5 A4
Reynalton 2 G5/5 A4
Reynoldston 6 E6
Rhadmad 4 F2
Rhandirmwyn 4 H5
Rhos 3 D6
Rhos-Hill 3 B6
Rhoscrowther 2 E5
Rhosmaen 6 G2
Rhossili 5 D6
Rhosson 1 C2
Rhyd-Rosser 4 F3
Rhyd-y-fro 6 H4
Rhydargaeau 6 E1
Rhydcymerau 4 F6
Rhydlewis 3 D5
Rhydowen 4 E5
Rhydwrach 2 H3/5 B2
Rinaston 2 F2
Roberston Cross 2 E4
Roberston Wathen 2 G4/5 A3
Roch 2 E3
Rosebush 2 G2/5 A1
Rosemarket 2 F5
Sageston 2 G5
Salem 6 G2
Sandfields 6 H6

Sarnau 5 C2
Saron 6 F3
Saundersfoot 2 H5/5 A4
Scleddau 2 F1
Scolton 2 F3
Scurlage 6 E6
Silian 4 F5
Siloh 4 H6
Simpson Cross 2 E3
Sketty 6 G6
Solva 1 D3
Southgate 6 F6
Spittal 2 F3
Square and Compass 2 E2
St. Brides 1 D4
St. Clears 5 C3
St. David's 1 C2
St. Dogmaels 3 A5
St. Florence 2 G5/5 A5
St. Ishmael 5 D4
St. Ishmael's 1 D5
St. Nicholas 2 E1
St. Petrox 2 F6
St. Twynnells 2 F6
Stackpole 2 F6
Star 5 B1
Steyton 2 E5
Strata Florida 4 H3
Swansea 6 G6
Swyddffynnon 4 G3
Taibach 6 H6
Tal-sarn 4 F5
Talbenny 1 D4
Talgarreg 3 D5
Talley 6 G1
Talog 5 C2
Tan-y-groes 3 C5
Tavernspite 2 H4/5 B3
Tegryn 2 H3/5 B1
Temple Bar 4 F4
Templeton 2 H4/5 A3
Tenby 2 H6/5 A5
The Mumbles 6 G6
Thomas Chapel 2 G5/5 A4
Three Crosses 6 F5
Tiers Cross 2 E4
Tonna 6 H5

Trapp 6 G2
Trn-groes 3 D5
Trecwn 2 F2
Trefenter 4 G2
Treffgarne 2 F2
Treffynnon 2 E2
Trefilan 4 F4
Trellän 1 D2
Trefin 1 D2
Tregaron 4 G3
Treglemais 1 D2
Trelech 5 C1
Treleddig-fawr 1 D2
Tremain 3 B5
Tresaith 3 C5
Tresinwen 1 D1
Tretio 1 D2
Trimsaran 6 E4
Troedyraur 3 C5
Tufton 2 G2
Tumble 6 F3
Twynllanan 6 H2
Ty-nant 4 H4
Tycroes 6 G4
Tynygraig 4 H2
Upper Cwm-twrch 6 H3
Upper Killay 6 F6
Uzmaston 2 F4
Wallis 2 F2
Walton East 2 F3
Walton West 2 E4
Walwyn's Castle 2 E4
Warren 2 F6
Waterston 2 F5
Waunarlwydd 6 F5
Welsh Hook 2 F2
West Cross 6 G6
West Williamston 2 G5
Whitchurch 1 D2
Whitland 5 B3
Wiston 2 G3
Wolfs Castle 2 F2
Wolfsdale 2 F3
Yerbeston 2 G5
Ysbyty Cynfyn 4 H1
Ysbyty Ystwyth 4 H2
Ystalyfera 6 H3
Ystrad Aeron 4 F4
Ystradmeurig 4 H2
Ystradowen 6 H3

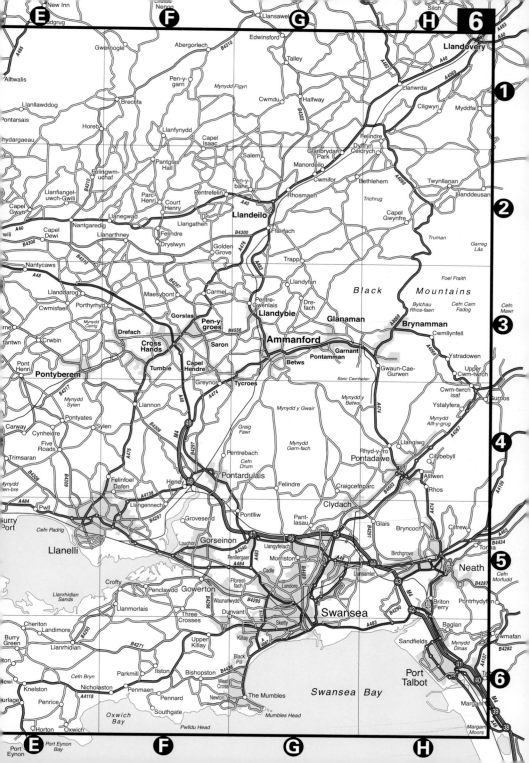

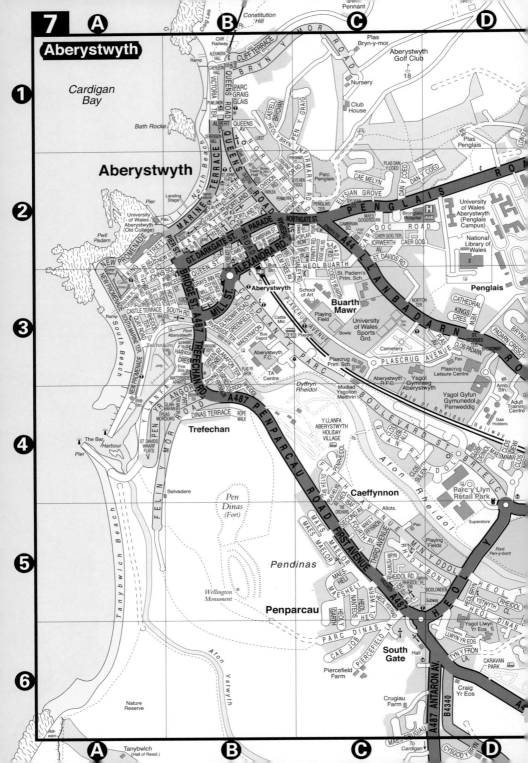

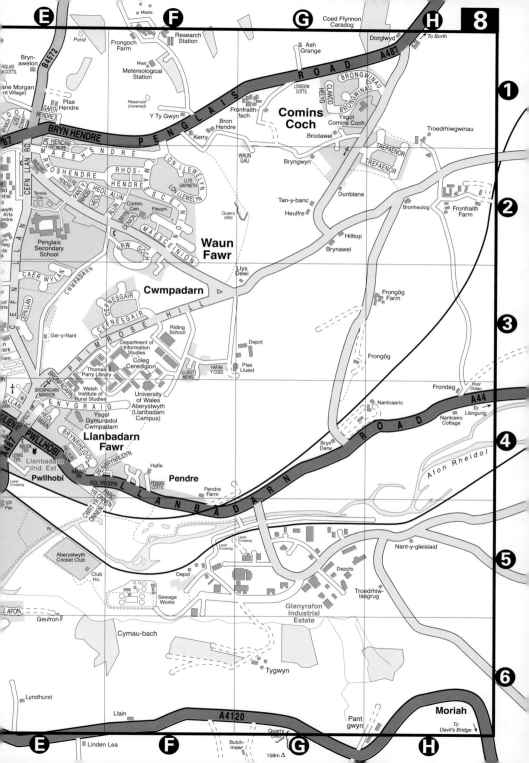

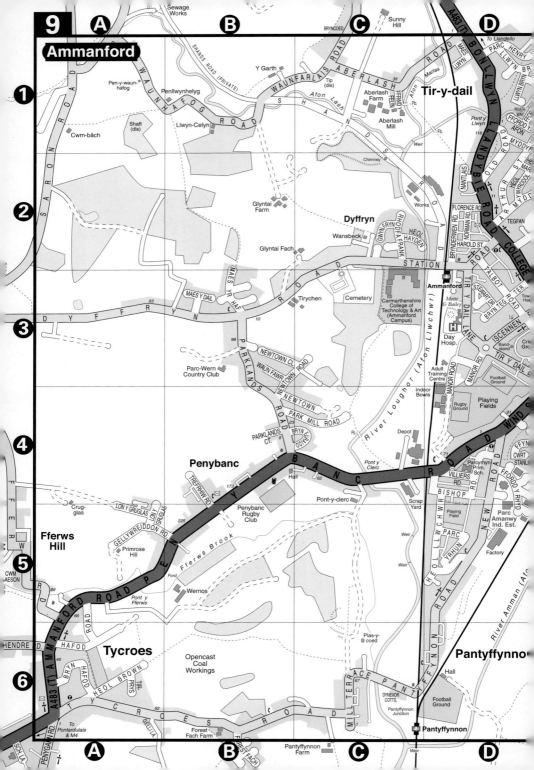

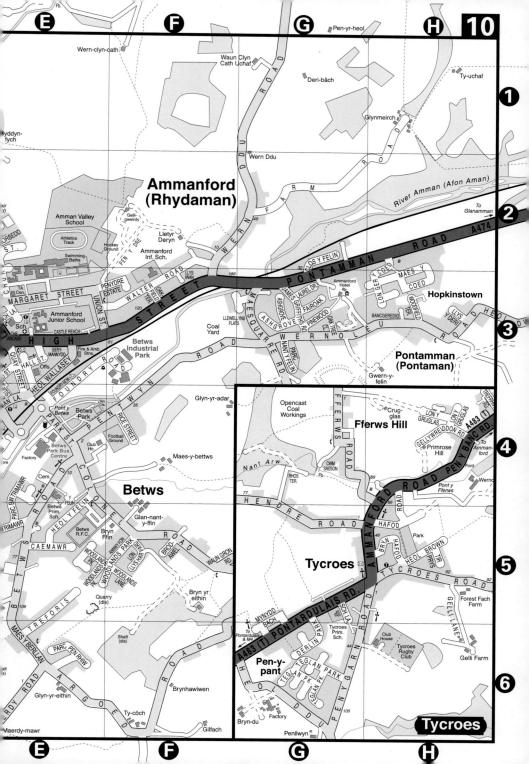

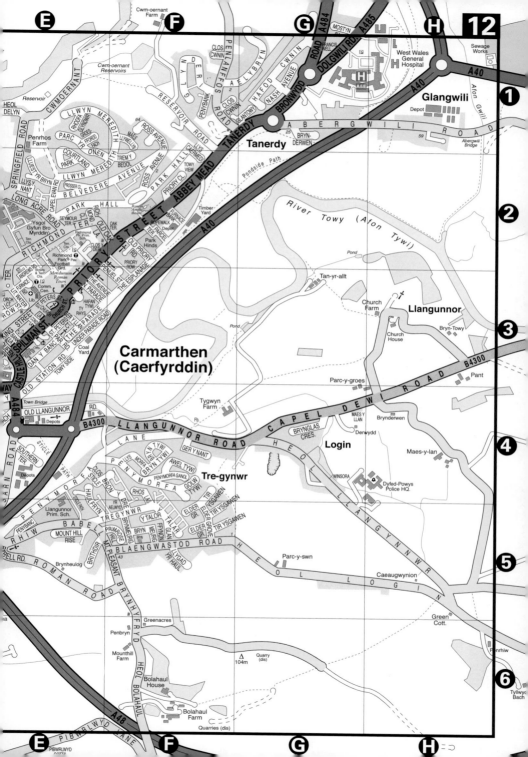

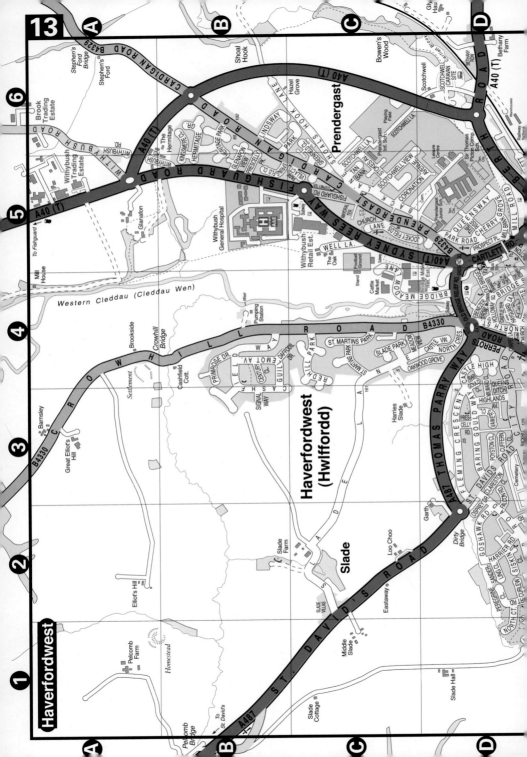

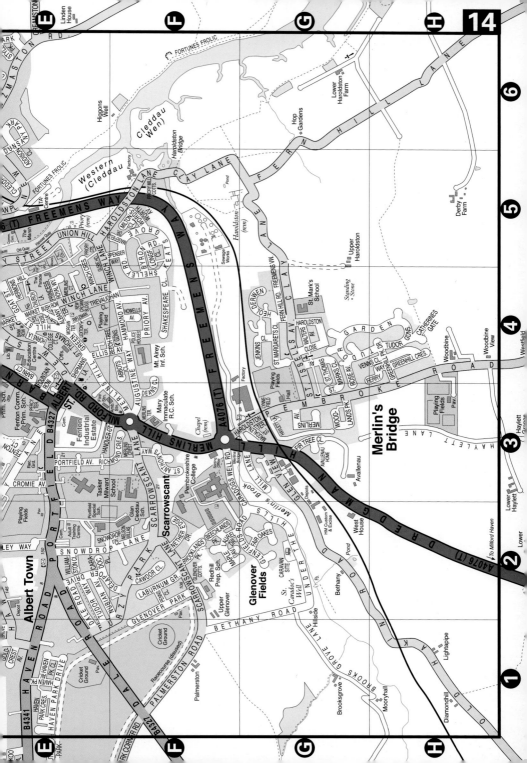

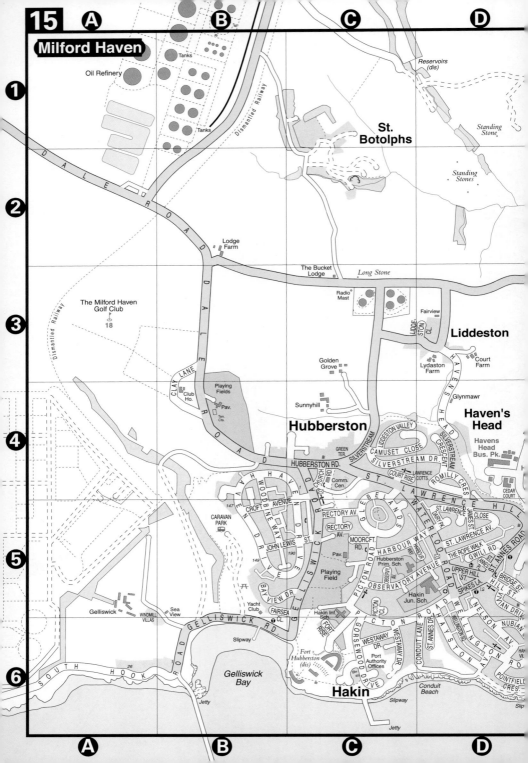

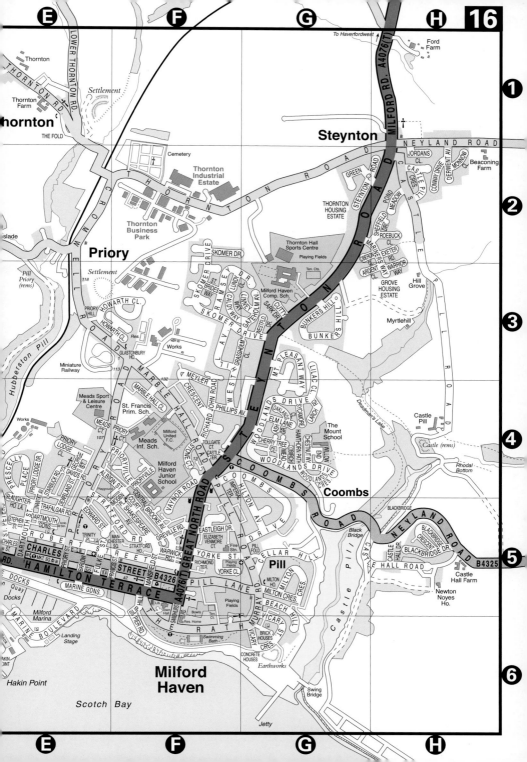

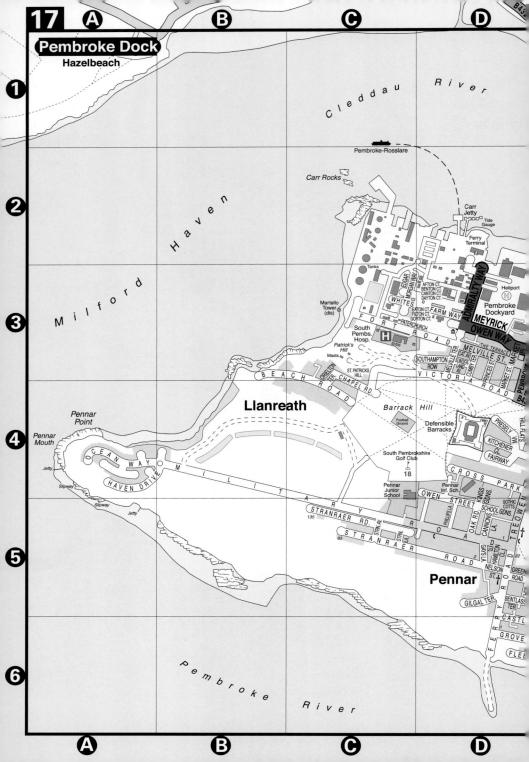

Pembroke Dock
Hazelbeach

Cleddau   River

Milford   Haven

Pembroke-Rosslare

Carr Rocks

Carr Jetty

Tide Gauge

Ferry Terminal

Tanks

AFTON CT.
BENTON CT.
CANTON CT.
DAYTON CT.

EDGAR

MORGAN WAY

WHITES

EATON CT.
FILTON CT.
GORTON CT.

ADMIRALTY WAY

Heliport

Pembroke Dockyard

MEYRICK

OWEN WAY

Martello Tower (dis)

PATERCHURCH

FORT ROAD

FARM WAY

THE TERRACE

PEMBROKE

MELVILLE ST.

South Pembs. Hosp.

H

MELVILLE

PRINCES ST.

MARKET ST.

MARKET

Patrick's Hill

SOUTHAMPTON ROW

CAT. AV.
SLADERS
CUMBY
LAND

VICTORIA ROAD

B.4.

Masts

ST. PATRICKS HILL

CHAPEL RD.

ORIEL TON

BEACH   ROAD

Llanreath

Barrack Hill

Football Ground

Defensible Barracks

PRESELY VW.

KITCHENER CL.

FAIRWAY

HILL FLATS

PRESELY

CROSS PARK

Pennar Point

Pennar Mouth

Jetty

OCEAN   WAY

HAVEN DRIVE

Slipway

Slipway

Jetty

M   I   L   I   T   A   R   Y

South Pembrokeshire Golf Club

18

Pennar Junior School

Pennar Inf. Sch.

135

STRANRAER RD.

STN. AV.

STRL

STRL ST.

OWEN   STREET

SCHOOL GDNS.

GOTHIC COTTS.

KINGS

CANONS LA.

PENINSULA

OAK RD.

TREOWEN

83

S   T   R   A   N   R   A   E   R   ROAD

GREEN ROAD

GANS ST.

HAMILTON

23

NELSON ST.

D

22

2

Pennar

GILGAL TER.

BENTLASS TER.

CASTL

GROVE

FERR

FLEE

Pembroke   River

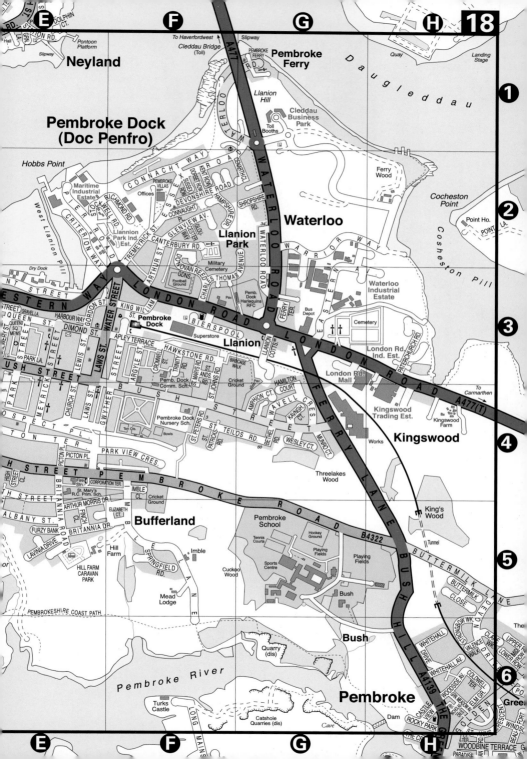

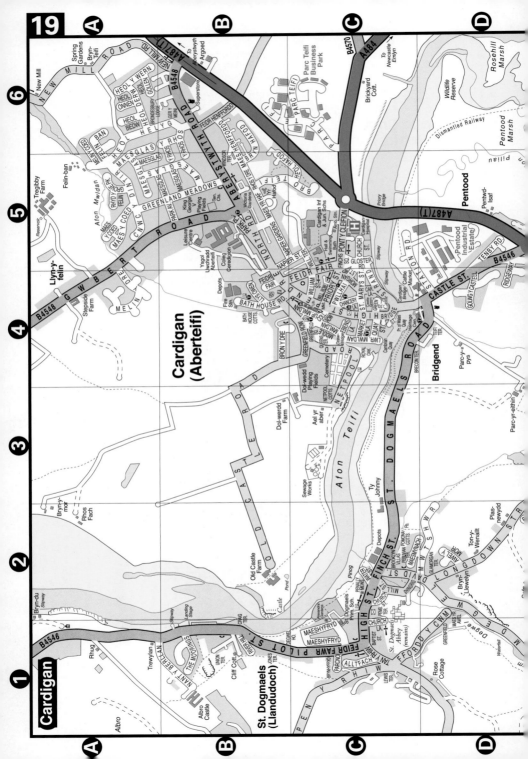

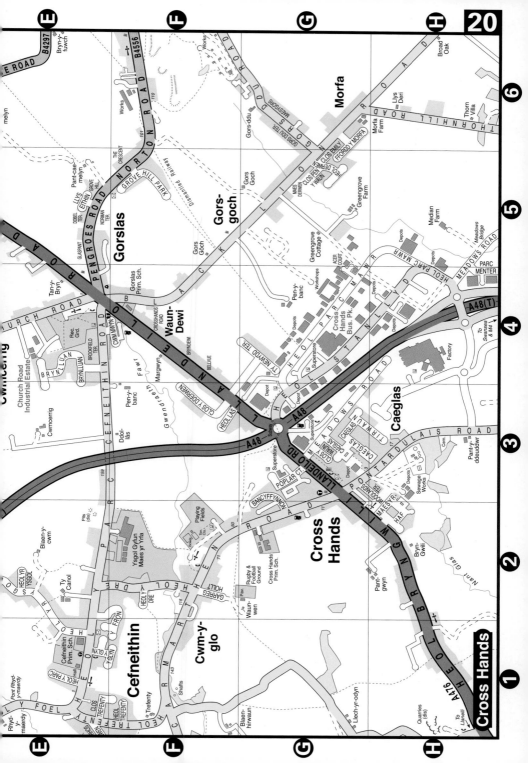

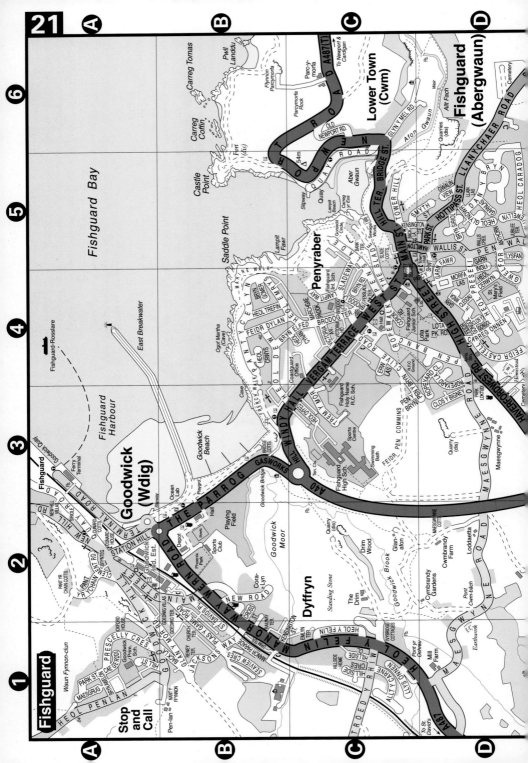

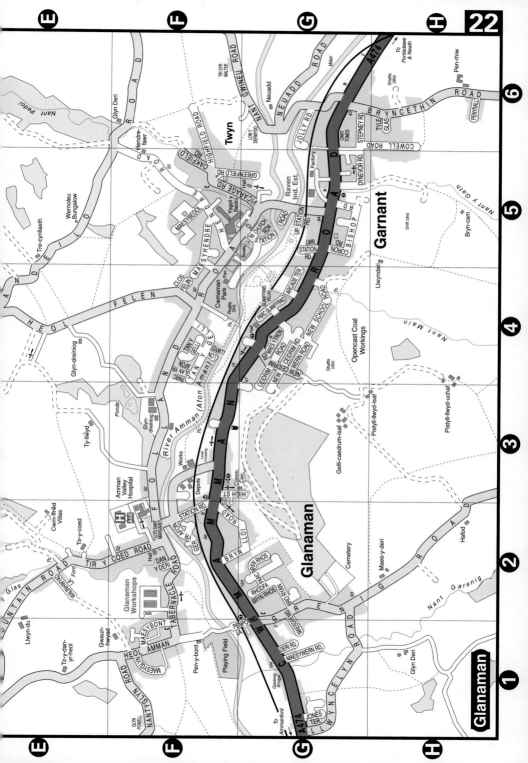

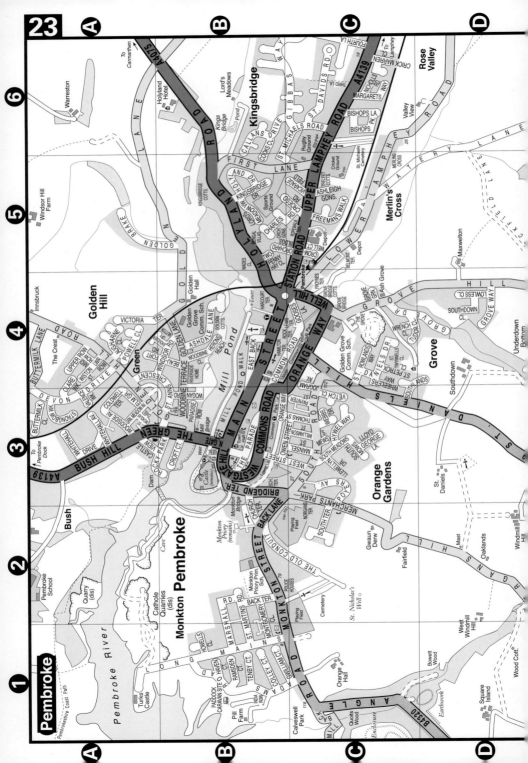

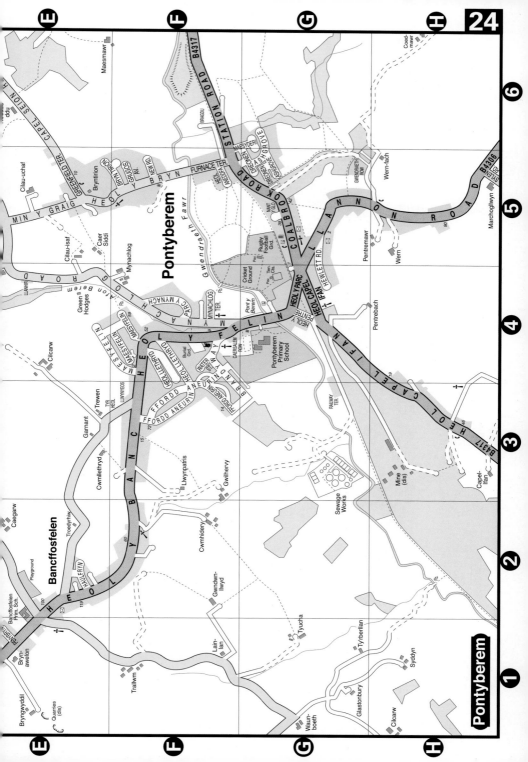

Pontyberem

Bancffosfelen

Maesmawr

Clîau-uchaf

Clîau-isaf

Caer Siddi

Mynachlog

Green Hodges

Cilcarw

Trewen

Garnant

Caegarw

Troedyrhiw

Cwmllethryd

Llwynpatris

Gwilherwy

Cwmhidery

Gwndwn-llwyd

Lain-lan

Trallwm

Bryngwyddil

Quarries (dis)

Bryn-awelon

Bancffosfelen Prim. Sch.

CAPEL SEION

GREENFIELD TER.

HEOL

MIN Y GRAIG

BRYN NON

GRUGOS AV.

BRYN

NEW RD.

FURNACE TER.

B4317

STATION ROAD

COALBROOK ROAD

BRAGDU

MAESYDERI

ASH GROVE

DRENEWI

GWENDRAETH ROW

Wern-fach

B4306

Marchogllwyn

LLANNON ROAD

Pentremawr

Wern

Pentrebach

Pentrebach

Coed-mawr

HEOL Y MYNACH

Afon Berem

Gwendraeth Fawr

MYNACHLOG TER.

PARK Y PARC

Pont y Berem

MAES FELIN

TYR HEOL

MAES FELIN

HEOL LLETHRI

HEOL LETHRI

LLWYNDDU

FFORDD ANEURIN

FFORDD ANEURIN

BANC-Y-WAY

Burial Grd.

WATER

CAERSALEM ROW

Pontyberem Primary School

HEOL Y FELIN

HEOL Y PARC

HEOL CAPEL

PENTRE

HEWLETT RD.

HEOL IFAN

RAILWAY TER.

HEOL CAPEL IFAN

B4317

Rugby Football Grd.

Cricket Ground

Sewage Works

Mine (dis)

Capel-Ifan

HEOL Y BANC

Hen Cts.

Tyucha

Tyberllan

Syddyn

Cilcarw

Glastonbury

Waun-boeth

Pontyberem

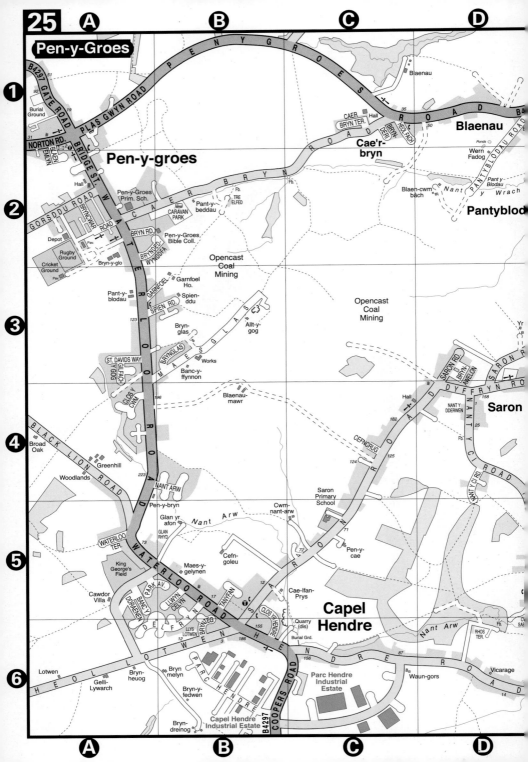

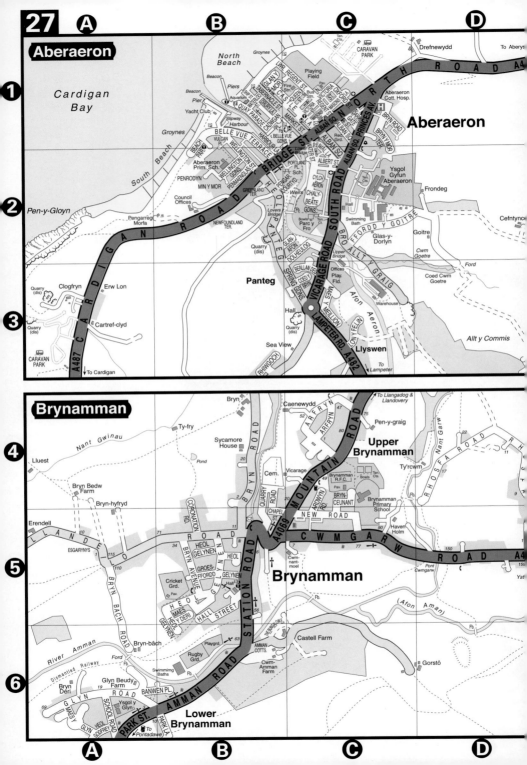

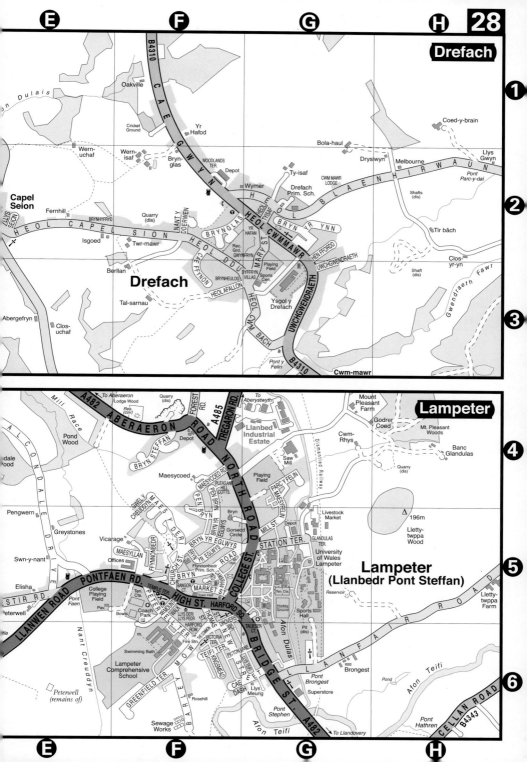

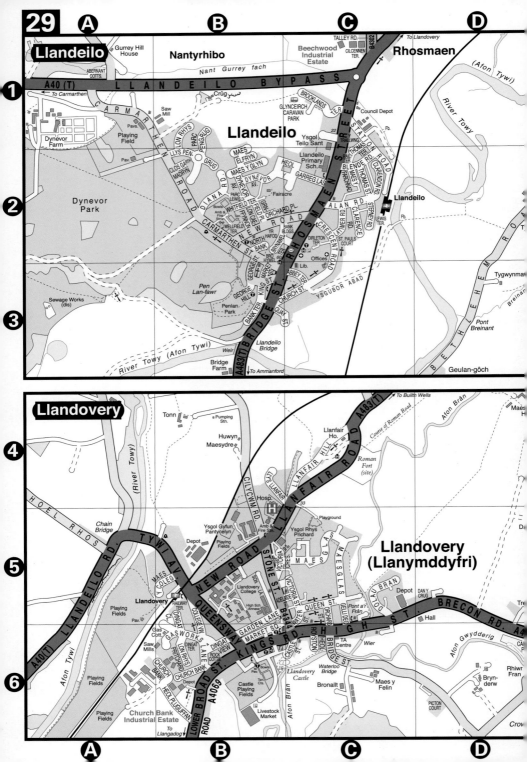

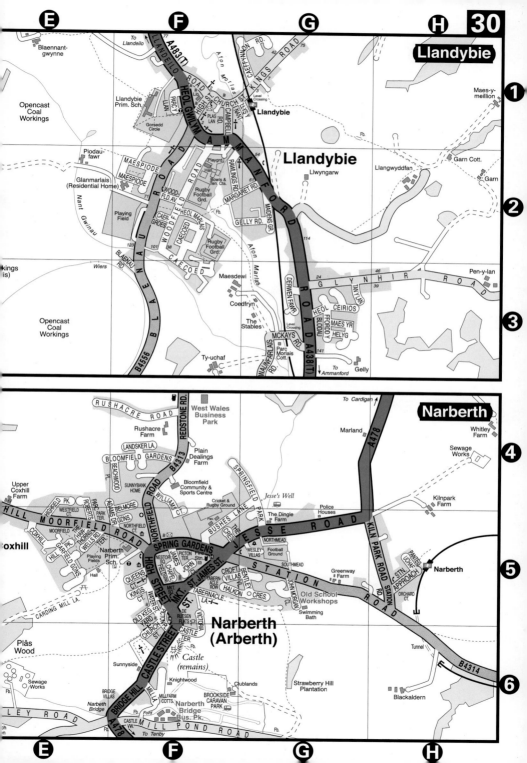

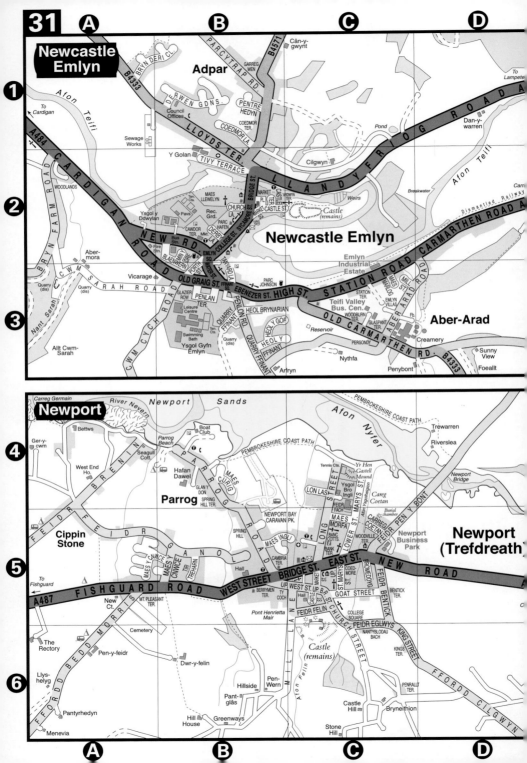

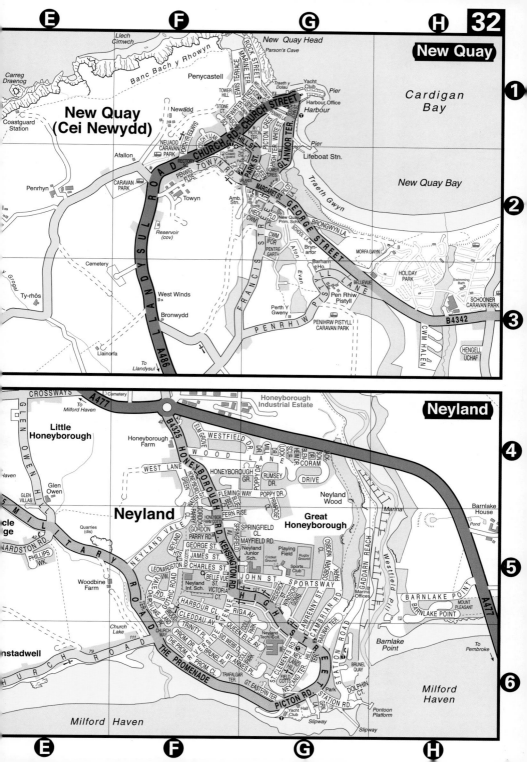

New Quay

Neyland

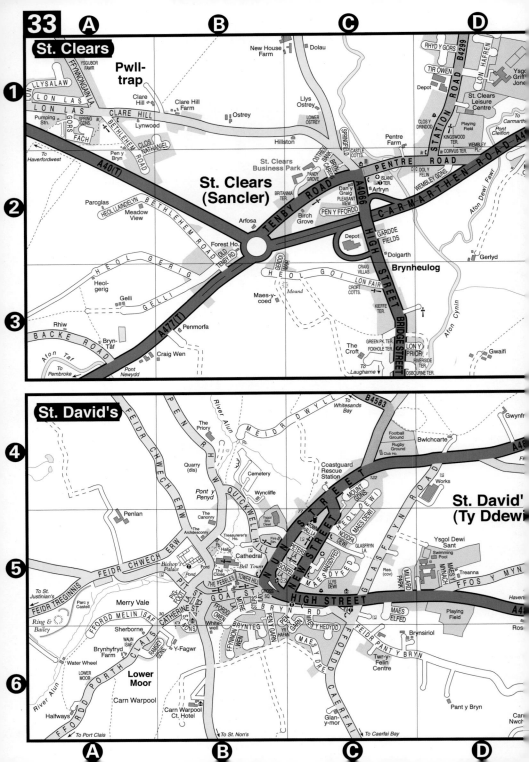

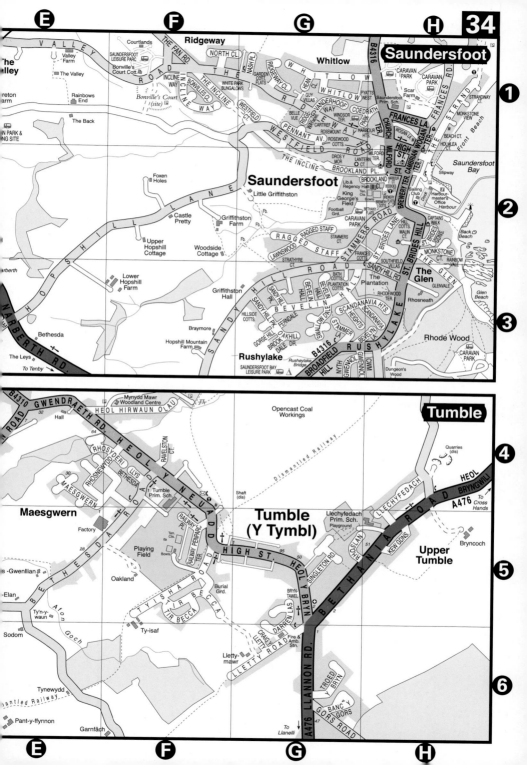

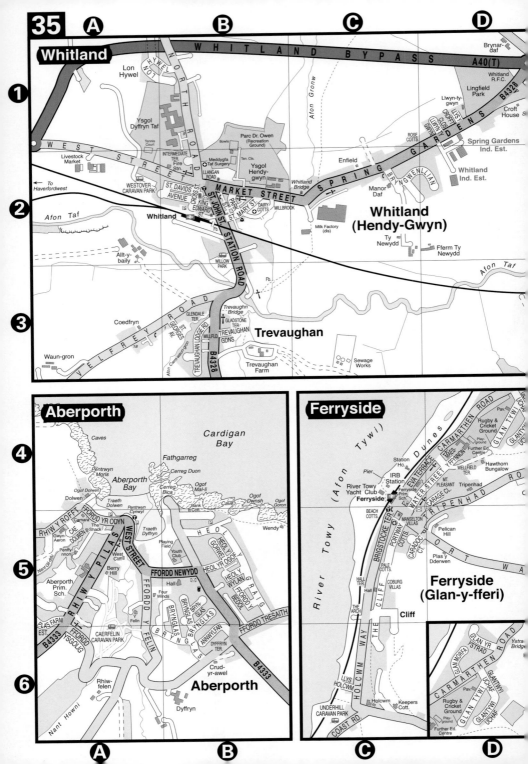

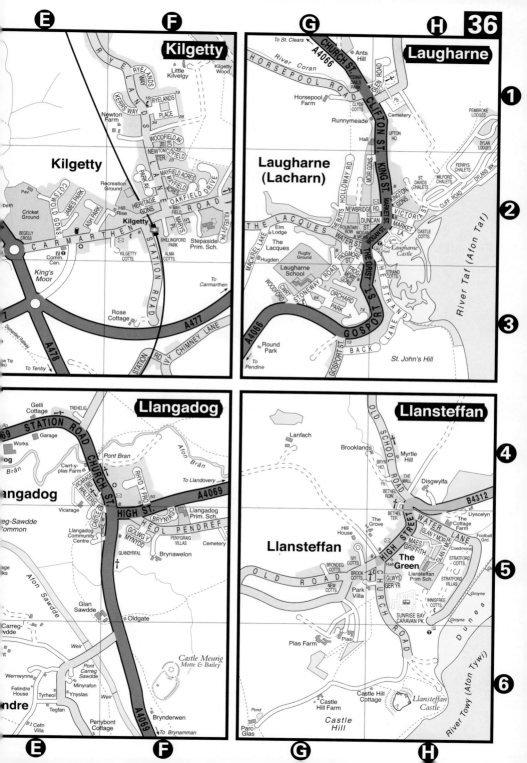

Kilgetty

Kilgetty

Little Kilvelgy
Kilgetty Wood
RYELANDS WAY
KERRS WAY
RYELANDS PLACE
Newton Farm
WOODFIELD AV.
WOODFIELD
NEWTON TER.
MAYFIELD ACRES
PARK AV.
HERITAGE GDNS.
OAKFIELD DRIVE
MAY. FIELD ACRES
ST. MARYS
Hill Rise
COTS. WOOD GDNS
JAMES PARK
ASH PARK
COLD GDNS
CARMARTHEN ROAD
Pav.
Cricket Ground
Recreation Ground
Kilgetty
beth
Begelly Cross
Comm. Cen.
King's Moor
Domestead Railway
KILGETTY PK.
Shillingford Park
Stepaside Prim. Sch.
ALMA COTTS.
Kilgetty Cotts.
STATION ROAD
IVY CHIMNEY LANE
STATION RD.
A478
To Tenby
A477
Rose Cottage
To Carmarthen

Laugharne

Laugharne (Lacharn)

To St. Clears
A4066
River Coran
CHURCH ST.
HORSEPOOL ROAD
CLIFTON ST.
KING ST.
Ants Hill
EDINA
DAILS
PARK
Fb.
CLYDE COTTS.
PEMBROKE LODGES
Horsepool Farm
Cemetery
UPTON HO.
DYLAN LODGES
FERRYS CHALETS
MILFORD CHALETS
ST. DAVIDS CHALETS
Runnymeade
Hall
SNO. BROW
HOLLOWAY RD.
NEWBRIDGE RD.
THE LACQUES
MACKREL LANE
Elm Lodge
The Lacques
Hugden
DUNCAN
FOUNTAIN ROW
WOGAN ST.
KINGSLAND
VICTORIA ST.
ST. DAVIDS CHALETS
DYLANS WK.
CLIFF ROAD
River Taf (Afon Taf)
MARKET
MARKET LA.
CASTLE COTTS.
Laugharne Castle
FROGMORE ST.
WATER ST.
THE GRIST
THE STRAND
STRAND COTTS.
Laugharne School
STONEWAY ROAD
CWRT WOODFORD
FROGMORE GDNS.
ORCHARD PARK
Rugby Ground
GOSPORT ST.
GOSPORT ST.
BACK LANE
A4066
Round Park
To Pendine
St. John's Hill

Llangadog

Llangadog

Gelli Cottage
TREHELIG
STATION ROAD
Works
Garage
CHURCH ST.
Pont Bran
Afon Brân
A4069
og
Brân
Cwrt-y-plas Farm
VICARAGE RD.
CASTLE RD.
WALTERS RD.
RHYD Y FRO
HIGH ST.
HEOL PENDREF
To Llandovery
A4069
Vicarage
BRYNIN
GOLWG Y MYNYDD
Llangadog Prim. Sch.
PENYGRAIG VILLAS
Cemetery
eg-Sawdde Common
Llangadog Community Centre
GLANDYRFAL
Brynawelon
Glan Sawdde
Oldgate
Afon Sawdde
Carreg-wdde
Weir
Wernwynne
Pont Carreg Sawdde
Minyrafon
Ynyslas
Weir
Castle Meurig Motte & Bailey
Felindre House
Tyrheol
Tegfan
Cefn Villa
Penybont Cottage
Brynderwen
To Brynamman
dre

Llansteffan

Llansteffan

Lanfach
OLD SCHOOL ROAD
Brooklands
BRYN HO.
Myrtle Hill
Disgwylfa
THE MALL
BETHEL ROW
B4312
Llyscelyn
The Cottage Farm
Hill House
The Grove
BETHEL TER.
WATER LANE
GLAN Y MOR
MAES GRIFFITH
GLAN Y MOR
Coedmore
Football Grd.
STRATFORD COTTS.
OLD ROAD
HIGH STREET
CHURCH ROAD
IVY COTTS.
BROOK COTTS.
Hall
EGLWYS GER YR
The Green
Llansteffan Prim. Sch.
STRATFORD VILLAS
BRONDEG COTTS.
NEW COTTS.
Park Villa
INNISFREE COTTS.
SUNRISE BAY CARAVAN PK.
Groyne
Groyne
Plas Farm
Plas
Dunes
Pond
Castle Hill Farm
Castle Hill Cottage
Llansteffan Castle
Parc Glas
Castle Hill
River Towy (Afon Tywi)

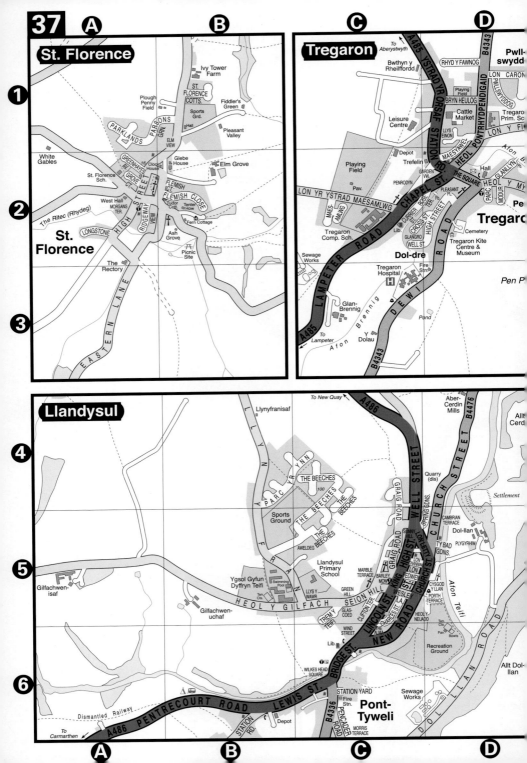

INDEX Abbreviations used

Abbr		Abbr		Abbr		Abbr		Abbr		Abbr	
Amb.	Ambulance	Comm.	Community	Flts.	Flats	Jun.	Junior	Orch(s).	Orchard(s)	Sq.	Square
App.	Approach	Comp.	Comprehensive	Fb.	Footbridge	La.	Lane	Par.	Parade	Stn.	Station
Arc.	Arcade	Crn.	Corner	Gdns.	Gardens	Lib.	Library	Pk.	Park	St.	Street
Av.	Avenue	Cott(s).	Cottage(s)	Gt.	Great	Lit.	Little	Pass.	Passage	Ten.	Tennis
Br.	Bridge	Cres.	Crescent	Grn.	Green	Lwr.	Lower	Pav.	Pavilion	Ter.	Terrace
Bldgs.	Buildings	Cft.	Croft	Grd.	Ground	Mkt.	Market	Pl.	Place	Up.	Upper
Bung(s).	Bungalow(s)	Ct.	Court	Gr.	Grove	Mag.	Magistrates	Prim.	Primary	Vic.	Vicarage
Bus.	Business	Dis.	Disused	Hd.	Head	Mdw(s).	Meadow(s)	Rec.	Recreation	Vw.	View
Cara.	Caravan	Dr.	Drive	Ho.	House	Mem.	Memorial	Res.	Reservoir	Vlls.	Villas
Cem.	Cemetery	E.	East	Hosp.	Hospital	Mon.	Monument	Resid.	Residential	Wk.	Walk
Cen.	Centre	Ent.	Enterprise	Ind.	Industrial	Mt.	Mount	Rd.	Road	Wy.	Way
Cl.	Close	Est.	Estate	Inf.	Infant	N.	North	Sch.	School	W.	West
Coll.	College	Fld(s).	Field(s)	Junc.	Junction	Off(s).	Office(s)	S.	South	Yd.	Yard

MYNEGAI Byrfoddau a ddefnyddir

Abbr		Abbr		Abbr		Abbr		Abbr		Abbr	
Amb.	Ambiwlans	Comm.	Cymuned	Flts.	Fflatiau	Jun.	Iau	Orch(s).	Perllan(-nau)	Sq.	Sgwar
App.	Dynesiad	Comp.	Cyfun	Fb.	Pont i gerddwyr	La.	Lon	Par.	Rhodfa	Stn.	Gorsaf
Arc.	Arced	Crn.	Congl	Gdns.	Gerddi	Lib.	Llyfrgell	Pk.	Parc	St./Str.	Stryd
Av.	Rhodfa	Cott(s).	Bwthyn(bythynnod)	Gt.	Mawr	Lit.	Bach	Pass.	Tramwyfa	Ten.	Tennis
Br.	Pont	Cres.	Cilgant	Grn.	Maes	Lwr.	Isaf	Pav.	Pafiliwn	Ter.	Terras
Bldg(s).	Adeiladau	Cft.	Tyddyn	Grd.	Maes	Mkt.	Marchnad	Pl.	Plas	Up.	Uchaf
Bung(s).	Byngalo(s)	Ct.	Llys	Gr.	Llwyn	Mag.	Ynad	Prim.	Cynradd	Vic.	Ficerdy
Bus.	Busnes	Dis.	Nis defnyddir	Hd.	Pen	Mdw(s).	Meadow(s)	Rec.	Hamdden	Vw.	Golygfa
Cara.	Carafan	Dr.	Rhodfa	Hosp.	Ysbyty	Mem.	Coffadwriaeth	Res.	Llyn	Vlls.	Filas
Cem.	Mynwent	E.	Dwyrain	Ind.	Diwydiannol	Mon.	Cofadail	Resid.	Preswyl	Wk.	Rhodfa
Cen.	Canolfan	Ent.	Anturiaeth	Inf.	Babanod	Mt.	Mynydd	Rd./Ff.	Heol/Ffordd	Wy.	Ffordd
Cl.	Clos	Est.	Ystad	Junc.	Cyffordd	N.	Gogledd	Sch.	Ysgol	W.	Gorllewin
Coll.	Coleg	Fld(s).	Cae(-au)			Off(s).	Swyddfa(-fedd)	S.	De	Yd.	Iard

Use of this Index: An alphabetical order is followed.

1. Each street name is followed by a map reference giving a page number and coordinates: Albert Street **27** C2.
2. Where a street name appears more than once the reference is given: Brynglas **35** B5/B6.
3. Names not appearing on the map are shown with an * and given the reference of the nearest adjoining street: Clos Ceitho*, Maesmawr **7** D4.
4. House numbers along streets are shown: 250.

Sut i ddefnyddio'r: Dilynnir trefn yr wyddor.

*Dilynnir enw pob stryd gan gyfeiriad map yn rhoi rhif tudalen a chyfesurynnau: Albert Street **27** C2.*

*Lle ymddengys enw stryd fwy nag unwaith rhoddir y cyfeiriad: Brynglas **35** B5/B6.*

*Dangosir enwau ni ymddangosir ar y map efo * a chyfeirnod at y stryd cydffiniol agosaf: Clos Ceitho*, Maesmawr **7** D4.*

Dangosir rhifau'r tai ar hyd y strydoedd: 250.

ABERAERON

Alban Square	27 C1/C2
Albert Street	27 C2
Beach Parade	27 B2
Belle Vue Gardens	27 B1
Belle Vue Terrace	27 B1
Berllan Deg	27 C3
Bridge Street	27 B1
Bro Allt y Graig	27 C2
Bryn Road	27 C1
Bryn y Mor Terrace	27 C1
Cadwgan Place	27 B1
Cardigan Road	27 A3
Castle Lane	27 C1
Chalybeate Gardens	27 C2
Coed y Bryn	27 C3
Cylch Aeron	27 C2
Dark Gate Street	27 C1
Dolheulog	27 C2
Drury Lane	27 B1
Ffordd y Goitre	27 C2
Glan y Mor	27 B1
Glanafon	27 C2
Greenland Terrace	27 B2
Harbour Lane	27 B1
Heol Panteg	27 C2
Lampeter Road	27 C3
Lon y Felin	27 C3
Lower Regent Street	27 C1
Maes y Meillion	27 C3
Market Street	27 C1
Masons Lane	27 C1
Masons Row	27 C1
Min y Mor	27 B2
Newfoundland Terrace	27 B2
North Road	27 C1
North Victoria Street	27 C1
Oxford Street	27 C1
Pengarreg Courtyard	27 B2
Penial Lane	27 C1
Penmaenglas	27 B2
Penrodyn	27 B2
Portland Place	27 C2
Princes Avenue	27 C1
Quay Parade	27 B1
Queen Street	27 C1
Regent Street	27 C1
Rhiwgoch	27 B3
Ship Street	27 B1
South Road	27 C2
Spring Gardens	27 C3
Tabernacle Street	27 B1
Vicarage Road	27 C3
Victoria Street	27 B1
Vulcan Place	27 B1
Water Street	27 C2
Waterloo Street	27 B1
Wellington Street	27 B2

ABERPORTH

Annwylfan	35 B6
Brynglas	35 B5/B6
Cae Dolwen	35 A5
Dyffryn Terrace	35 B6
Ffordd Newydd	35 B6
Ffordd Tresaith	35 B6
Ffordd Ysgolig	35 A6
Ffordd y Bedol	35 B5
Ffordd y Felin	35 A5
Ffordd yr Odyn	35 A5
Heol y Gorwel	35 B5
Heol y Graig	35 A5
Heol y Wylan	35 B5
Heol yr Ogof	35 B5
Plas Farm Estate	35 A5
Rhiw y Pilas	35 A5
Rhiw y Rofft	35 A5
West Street	35 A5

ABERYSTWYTH

Albert Place	7 B1
Albion Cottages	7 B3
Alexandra Hall	7 B1
Alexandra Road	7 B2
Alfred Place	7 B2
Antaron Avenue	7 D6
Baker Street	7 B2
Banadl Road	7 C2
Beehive Terrace	7 B4
Bilston Terrace	8 E4
Bodlondeb	7 D5
Boulevard St. Brieuc	7 C4
Brewer Street	7 B2
Bridge Street	7 B3
Bridge Terrace*, Ff. Sulien	8 E4
Bridgend Cottages	7 B3
Broadway	7 D4
Brongwinau	8 G1
Brongpadarn	8 E4
Brook Terrace	8 F2
Bryn Ceinion	8 G1
Bryn Derw*, Stanley Road	7 D3
Bryn Hendre	8 E1
Bryn Place	7 C5
Bryn Rheidol	8 E4
Bryn y Mor Road	7 B1
Bryn y Mor Terrace	7 B1
Bryn yr Eglwys*, Greys Inn Road	7 B3
Bryn Ysgol*, Heol Bryn	7 D5
Bryn Ystwyth	7 C5
Brynglas Road	7 D3
Cae Job	7 C6
Cae Melyn	7 C2
Caer Gog	7 C2
Caer Gog Terrace	7 C2
Caer Wylan	8 E3
Caerleon Hall	7 B1
Cambrian Place	7 B2
Cambrian Square	7 C2
Cambrian Street	7 B2
Cambridge Terrace	7 B2
Caradoc Road	7 C2
Castle Street	7 A2
Castle Terrace	7 A3
Cathedral View	7 D3
Cefn Llan	8 E3
Cefn Llan Road	8 E2
Cefnesgair	8 F3
Ceredigion Hall	7 B1
Chalybeate Street	7 B2
Church Street*, Heol y Llan	8 E4
Clas Deiniol	7 D4
Clawdd Helyg	8 G1
Cliff Terrace	7 B1
Clos Ceitho*, Maesmawr	7 D4
Clos Dewi	7 D4
Clos Gerwallt	7 C4
Clos Padarn	7 D3
Clos Penri*, Thespian St.	7 B2
Clos Sulien	7 C4
Coed y Boarth	7 B3
Coedlan y Parc	7 B3
Cogerddan Cottages	7 C2
Corporation Street	7 B2
Custom House Street	7 A3
Cwmpadarn	8 E3

Cwrt yr Angor.....

Cwrt yr Angor 7 B4
Cwrt yr Onnen 8 E5
Cynfryn Buildings 7 B2
Cysgod y Bryn 7 D6
Dan y Coed 7 C2
Dinas Terrace 7 B4
Eastgate 7 B2
Edge Hill Road 7 C2
Elm Tree Avenue 7 B2
Elysian Grove 7 C2
Erw Goch 8 F2
Fairlea 7 B1
Felin y Mor Road 7 A5
Felindre 8 E2
Ffordd Sulien 8 E4
Fifth Avenue 7 C4
First Avenue 7 C5
Fourth Avenue 7 C5
Garth Dinas 7 D6
Garth Hendre 8 E1
George Street 7 B3
Gerddi Ffynnon 7 B3
Gerddi Gwalia*, Portland Road
....7 B2
Gerddi Rheidol 7 A4
Glan Rheidol 7 C4
Glanhafan 7 A4
Glanrafon Terrace 7 B3
Glenhurst Villas 7 B3
Glyndwr Road 7 B3
Glynpadarn 7 D4
Gogerddan Cottages*,
     Penglais Road.................7 C2
Grays Inn Road 7 B3
Great Darkgate Street 7 B2
Green Gardens 7 B3
Greenfield Street 7 B3
Gwel Fron 8 E5
Gwel Rheidol*, Heol Bryn 7 D5
Hafon y Coed 8 F3
Harbour Crescent 7 B3
Haulwen 7 C5
Heol Alun 8 E2
Heol Bryn 7 D5
Heol Dinas 7 D5
Heol Isaf 7 C4
Heol Iwain 8 E4
Heol Nanteos 7 C5
Heol Rheidol 7 D1
Heol Tyn y Fron 7 D5
Heol y Bont 7 D5
Heol y Bryn 7 B1
Heol y Buarth 7 C2
Heol y Garth 7 C5
Heol y Llan 8 E4
Heol y Wern 7 C5
Heol Ystrad 7 C5
High Street 7 B3
Infirmary Road 7 C2
Iorwerth Avenue 7 C2
King Street 7 A2
Kings Crescent 7 D3
Laura Place 7 A2
Laurel Place 7 B2
Lewis Terrace 8 E4
Lisburne Terrace 7 B2
Llanbadarn Road 7 C3/8 F4
Lluest Mews 8 F3
Llwyn yr Eos 7 D6
Llys Gwyneth 8 F2
Llys Hen Brychan 7 B1
Llys Hendre 8 E2

Llys Mynach 8 E1
Lon Cleddau 7 D1
Lon Conwy 8 E1
Lon Dyfi 8 E1
Lon Hendre 8 E1
Lon Llewelyn 8 F2
Lon Teifi 7 D1
Lon Ystwyth 8 E1
Lovedon Cottages 8 G1
Lovedon Road 7 B2
Luest 7 B1
Maes Ceinion 8 F2
Maes Cogerddan 7 C2
Maes Crugiau 7 C6
Maes Maelor 7 C5
Maes y Ffynnon 7 C5
Maesheli 7 C5
Maeshendre 8 E2
Maesmawr 7 D4
Maesyrafon 7 B3
Marine Terrace 7 B2
Market Street 7 B3
Mill Street 7 B3
Min y Ddol 7 C5
Moor Lane 7 B3
New Promenade 7 A2/A3
New Street 7 A2
North Parade 7 B2
North Road 7 B1
Northgate Street 7 C2
Norton Terrace 7 C3
Orchard, The 7 C5
Padarn Crescent 7 D3
Padarn Lane 8 E4
Padarn Terrace 8 E4
Pant y Rhos 8 E2
Parc Dinas 7 C6
Parc Dolau 7 C5
Parc Graig Glais 7 B1
Parc yr Onnen 8 E4
Pen Maes Glas Road 7 A3
Pen y Fron Cottages 8 E3
Pen y Fron Road 8 E4
Pen y Graig 7 C1/8 E4
Penbrynrudyn 8 E4
Pendre Cottages 8 F4
Penglais Farm Cottages 8 E1
Penglais Road 7 C2/8 F1
Penglais Terrace 7 C2
Penheidol 7 C4
Penmorfa 7 B2
Penparcau Road 7 B4/C5
Pentre Jane Morgan
     Student Village 8 E1
Penygraig 8 E4
Penygraig Court 7 C2
Pier Street 7 B2
Piercefield Lane 7 C6
Plas Avenue 7 D3
Plas Dan y Coed 7 C2
Plas Helyg 7 C4
Plas Helyg Avenue 7 C5
Plas Iorwerth*, Caradoc Rd...7 C2
Plas Mair*, Grays Inn Road ..7 B3
Plas Morolwg 7 B4
Plas Newydd*, Queens St. ...7 B3
Plas Padarn 8 E4
Plas yr Afon 7 B3
Plascrug Avenue 7 B3/C3
Poplar Row 7 B2
Portland Road 7 B2
Portland Street 7 B2

Pound Place 7 C2
Powell Street 7 B3
Primrose Hill 8 E3
Princess Street 7 B3
Prospect Place 8 E4
Prospect Street 7 A3
Pumlumon 7 B1
Pwllhobi 8 E4
Pwllhobi Terrace 8 E4
Quay Road 7 A3
Quebec Row 7 D4
Queen Street 7 B3
Queens Avenue 7 B1
Queens Road 7 B1/B2
Railway View 8 E4
Rheidol Close 7 D5
Rheidol Place 7 C5
Rheidol Road 7 C5
Rheidol Terrace 7 A3
Rheidol View 7 C5
Rhoshendre 8 E2/F2
Rhybudd Student Village 8 E2
Rhyd y Bont 7 C5
Rhydyr Afon 7 B3
Riverside Terrace 7 B3
Rope Walk 7 B4
Sea View Place 7 A3
Second Avenue 7 C5
Side Street 7 C2
Skinner Street 7 C2
South Marine Terrace 7 A3
South Road 7 B3
Spring Gardens 7 B3
St. Davids Road 7 C2
St. Davids Wharf Flats 7 A4
St. Georges Terrace 7 D4
St. James Mews*, Castle St. ..7 A2
St. James Square 7 B3
St. Johns Flats 7 B2
St. Johns Square 7 A4
St. Michaels Place 7 A3
Stanley Road 7 C2
Stanley Terrace 7 B2
Swan Square 7 B2
Sylvan Court 7 B2
Terrace Road 7 B2
Thespian Street 7 B2
Third Avenue 7 C5
Trefaenor 8 H2
Trefechan Road 7 B3
Trefor Road 7 B2
Tremafon*, Heol Bryn 7 D5
Trinity Place 7 C2
Trinity Road 7 C2
Ty Mawr 8 E4
Tyn y Fron Close 7 D6
Tyn y Fron Lane 7 D6
Union Street 7 B2
Vaenor Street 7 B2
Victoria Terrace 7 B1
Vulcan Street 7 A3
Waterside Apartments 7 B3
Waun Fawr Cottages 8 E2
William Street 7 B3
Windmill Court*, Pier Street ..7 B2
Y Lanfa 7 A4
Y Llanfa Aberystwyth
     Holiday Village 7 C4
Yr Hen Sgubor*, Cambrian Street
....7 B2
Yr Odyn*, Pen yr Angor 7 B4
Ystwyth Close 7 D5

AMMANFORD

Aberlash Road 9 C1
Ammanford Road 9 A6/10 H5
Annwy Fron 10 F5
Arcade, The 10 E3
Argoed Road 10 E6
Arthur Street 10 E3
Ashgrove 10 G3
Bancgeredig 10 H3
Baptist Lane 10 E5
Betws Road 10 E5
Bishop Road 9 D4
Bonllwyn 9 D3
Brodawel 10 F5
Bryn Euraidd 9 D2
Bryn Hafod (Tycroes) ..9 A6/10 H5
Bryn Teg Terrace 9 D3
Bryncoed 9 C1
Brynderwen Road 9 D2
Brynmawr 9 D2
Brynmawr Avenue 9 D2
Brynmawr Lane 10 E5
Caemawr 10 E5
Carregamman 9 D4
Carregamman Isaf 10 F5
Carregamman Lane 10 E4
Castle Reach 10 E3
Church Street 10 E3
Clos y Felin 10 G2
College Street 10 D2
Colonel Road 10 E4
Coronation Terrace*,
     Maes Quarre Road 10 G3
Cross Inn Buildings 10 E3
Cwm Saeson (Tycroes) 10 G5
Cwrt Stanllyd 9 D4
Danycoed*, Pen y Banc Rd ..9 D4
Derlin Park (Tycroes) 10 G6
Dyffryn Road 9 A3
Dynevor Cottages 9 C6
Fairoak 10 G3
Farm Road 10 G2
Fferws Road (Tycroes) 10 G5
Ffordd y Rhyd 9 D4
Ffordd yr Afon 9 D1
Fforest Fach*, Tycroes Road
....10 H5
Ffrwd y Felin 9 C1
Ffynnon Las 9 D3
Florence Road 9 D2
Forest Fach Estate 9 D3
Foundry Road 10 E4
Foundry Row 10 E4
Gelli Lane 9 A6/10 H5
Gellywreiddon Road (Tycroes)
....9 A5/10 H4
Germannydd 10 E5
Glan yr Afon 9 D1
Gwaun Henllan 9 D1
Gwynfryn 9 C2
Hafod Road (Tycroes) 9 A6/10 H5
Hall Street 10 E3
Harold Street 9 D2
Hendre Road (Tycroes) 10 G4
Heol Brown (Tycroes) 9 A6/10 H5
Heol Ddu (Tycroes) 10 H3
Heol Dwr 9 C2
Heol Hayden 9 C2
Heol Las 9 D5
Heol Llwchwr 9 D5
Heol Llwyd 9 D1

Heol Marlais 9 D2
Heol Wallasey 10 E4
Heol y Felin 10 E5
Heol y Wyrddol 9 D2
High Street 10 E3
Iscennen Road 9 D3
James Griffiths Road 10 G3
Laurel Drive 10 G3
Llandybie Road..................9 D1
Lletyr Deryn 10 F2
Llewellyns Flats 10 G3
Llewellyns Yard*,
     Maes Quarre Road......10 G3
Lloyd Street........................10 E3
Llwyn Maes........................9 D1
Llwyn y Bryn 9 D1
Llys Iwan 10 F3
Llys y Deri 10 H3
Lon Ger y Coed 10 H3
Lon Llys Harvard 10 F5
Lon y Gruglas (Tycroes)
.............................9 A5/10 H4
Maerdy Road 10 E6
Maes Llwyn........................9 D1
Maes y Berllan 10 E6
Maes y Coed......................10 H3
Maes y Dail 9 B3
Maes yr Haf........................9 B3
Maesquarre Road..............10 G3
Manor Road 9 D3
Margaret Street..................10 E3
Mill Terrace 9 C6
Myddynfych 9 D1/D2
Mynydd Bach (Tycroes) ..10 G5
Nantlais 9 D2
New Road 9 D5
Newtown 9 B4
Newtown Close 9 B3
Newtown Road 9 B4
Norman Road 9 D2
Oak Tree Close 10 G3
Oakfield Terrace 10 F3
Old Road..............................9 D2
Pantyffynnon Road 9 C6
Parc Amanwy 9 D5
Parc Bwtrimawr................10 E5
Parc Henry Lane................9 D1
Parc Nant y Felin 10 G2
Parc Pen Rhiw 10 E6
Parcyrhun 9 D5
Park Mill Road....................9 B4
Park Street 10 E4
Parklands Court 9 B4
Parklands Road 9 B3
Pen y Banc Road 9 A5/10 H4
Pen y Dre 10 F2
Pentwyn Road 10 E4
Penydre Estate 10 F3
Penygarn Road (Tycroes) ..10 G6
Pinewood 10 G3
Pont Amman Road............10 G3
Pontardulais Road (Tycroes)
....10 G6
Quay Street........................10 E3
Rhodfa Frank......................9 C2
Rhos Terrace (Tycroes) 10 G5
Rice Street 10 F4
Riverway 9 D1
Saron Road 9 A2
School Lane 10 E3
Shands Road 9 B1/C1
Station Road 9 C2

Stewart Drive 9 D3
Talbot Road 9 D3
Tegfan..................................9 D2
Teglan Park (Tycroes) 10 G6
Tir y Dail Lane......................9 D3
Tirprys (Tycroes) 9 A6/10 H5
Treforis 10 E6
Trefrhiw Road............9 B4/10 H4
Tycroes Road 10 H5
Union Street 10 E3
Villiers Road 9 D4
Walter Road 10 F3
Waun Fawr 9 B3
Waun Gron Road 10 F5
Waunfarlais Road 9 B1
Waunhafog Road 9 A1
Wern Ddu Road 10 F2
Wernoleu Road 10 G3
Wind Street 9 D4
Woodfield Terrace 10 H3
Woodlands Lane 10 F5
Woodlands Park 10 F5
Y Felin 10 E4
Y Gorsedd 10 E2

BRYNAMMAN

Amman Cottages 27 B6
Amman Road 27 B6
Ardwyn Road 27 C5
Arfryn 27 C4
Banwen Place....................27 A6
Bryn Avenue 27 B5
Bryn Bach Road 27 A5
Bryn Road 27 B4
Brynceunant 27 C4
Bungalows, The 27 B6
Chapel Street 27 B5
Coronation Road................27 B5
Cwmgarw Road 27 C5
Esgairynys 27 A5
Glyn Road 27 A6
Groesffordd 27 B5
Hall Street 27 A6
Heol Gelynen 27 B5
Heol Godfrey......................27 A6
Llandeilo Road 27 C4
Maes y Deri 27 B5
Maes y Glyn 27 A6
Mountain Road 27 C4
New Road 27 C5
Park Lane 27 B6
Park Street 27 A6
Quarry Road 27 B4
Rhosfa Road 27 D4
School Road 27 A6
Station Road 27 B6

CARDIGAN
ABERTEIFI

Aberystwyth Road..............19 B5
Albion Terrace*, Lower Mwldan
....19 C4
Alltfach 19 C1
Awel y Mor 19 D2
Baptist Street 19 C1
Bath House Cottages 19 B4
Bath House Road 19 B4
Brecon Terrace 19 C4
Brick Row*, Strand 19 C4
Bridge Street 19 C4
Bro Teifi..............................19 C5

Bron y Dre..........................19 B4
Brondesbury Lodge 19 A6
Brooklyn Villas 19 C2
Bryn Hafod 19 B5
Bryngwyn 19 D2
Brynhyfryd..........................19 C1
Carriers Lane 19 C4
Castle Street 19 D4
Chancery Lane 19 C4
Church Lane 19 C1
Church Street (Cardigan) 19 C5
Church Street (St. Dogmaels)
....19 C2
Cnwc y Dintir......................19 A5
College Row 19 C4
Craig Terrace 19 B1
Cwmdegwell 19 D1
David Street 19 C2
Degwell House 19 B1
Ebens Lane........................19 C4
Feidr Fair 19 B4/C4
Feidr Fawr..........................19 C1
Feidr Henffordd 19 B6
Felin Ban............................19 A5
Fordd y Cwm 19 C1
Finch Street 19 C2
Finchs Square....................19 C5
Ger y Meini 19 B6
Glamorgan Terrace 19 D2
Gloster Road......................19 C5
Golwg y Castell..................19 C4
Green Street 19 C4
Greenfield 19 D1
Greenfield Row 19 C4
Greenfield Square 19 C4
Greenland Meadows 19 A5
Grove Park 19 A5
Gwbert Road......................19 A4
Heol Bedw..........................19 A6
Heol Derw 19 A6
Heol Gollen 19 A6
Heol Hafod 19 C5
Heol Helyg 19 A6
Heol Onnen........................19 A6
Heol y Wern 19 A6
High Street (Cardigan) 19 C4
High Street (St. Dogmaels) 19 C1
High Street Arcade*, High Street
....19 C4
Jones Terrace 19 B1
Lewis Terrace 19 C4
Llys Owen 19 B4
Longdown Street 19 D2
Lower Mwldan 19 C4
Maes Henffordd 19 B5
Maes y Coed......................19 A5
Maes yr Awel 19 A5
Maes yr Haf........................19 B5
Maesglas 19 A5/B5
Maeshyfryd 19 C1
Maesmynach 19 C2
Market Lane 19 C4
Melin y Coed 19 A5
Melin y Dre 19 A4
Middle Mwldan 19 C4
Mill Street 19 C4
Moorings,The 19 B1
Morgan Street 19 C4
Mwtshwr 19 D2
Nant y Berllan 19 B1
Napier Street 19 B5
Netpool Cottages 19 C3

Netpool Road 19 C3
New Mill Lane 19 A6
New Mill Road 19 A6/B6
North Road 19 B5
Old Castle Road 19 B2
Parc Teifi............................19 C6
Parcnoi 19 C1
Park Avenue 19 B5
Park Place..........................19 B5
Pembroke Terrace 19 C2
Pen y Rhiw 19 C1
Penally Mews 19 C2
Pendre 19 C4
Peruvian Terrace 19 C2
Pilot Street 19 C1
Pomona Cottages..............19 C2
Pont y Cleifion....................19 C5
Priory Court*, Priory Street..19 C4
Priory Street 19 C4
Pwllhai................................19 C4
Quay Street........................19 C4
Queens Terrace 19 C4
Rhos y Dre 19 B5
Rhyd y Felin 19 A5
Ridgeway 19 D4
River Hill 19 B1
Royal Oak 19 C4
Shingrig..............................19 C2
St. Dogmaels Road 19 C3
St. Mary Street 19 C4
St. Marys Cottages*, Feidr Fair
....19 C4
Station Road 19 D4
Strand 19 C4
Tan y Rhiw 19 C1
Teifi Terrace 19 D4
Tenby Road 19 D5
Union Terrace 19 B1
Upper Mwldan 19 C4
Water Street 19 C2
William Row 19 C4
William Street 19 C4
William Terrace..................19 C5
Windsor Terrace 19 B5
Y Rhos 19 B6

CARMARTHEN
CAERFYRDDIN

Abbey Mead 12 F2
Abergwili Road 12 G1
Aelybryn 12 F1
Albion Arcade 11 D3
Allt Ioan 11 A4
Allt y Gog............................11 A3
Alltycnap Road 11 A6
Amex Park 11 C5
Anthony Way......................11 A5
Ash Grove 11 B4
Avenue, The 12 E3
Awel Tywi 12 F4
Babell Road 12 E5
Bank Lane 12 E3
Barn Road..........................11 D3
Barnsfield Terrace 11 D3
Beech Road 11 B3
Belvedere Avenue 12 E2
Blaengwastod Road 12 F5
Blue Street 11 D3
Brewery Road 11 D2
Brickyard Lane 11 C4
Bridge Street......................12 E3

Brithdir.....

Brithdir.....................................12 E5
Bro Hedydd...............................11 D2
Bro Myrddin..............................11 B3
Bron y Dre................................12 F4
Bron yr Aur...............................11 B6
Bronwydd Road 12 G1
Bryn Gorwel..............................11 D2
Bryn Terrace............................12 F5
Bryn Tywi..................................12 F4
Brynderwen 12 G1
Brynglas Crescent 12 G4
Brynhaul Street 11 D2
Brynhyfryd................................12 F5
Brynmeurig 12 F5
Brynteg 11 A2
Bull Lane 11 D3
Bulwarks, The..........................11 D2
Cadifor Steet...........................11 D2
Cae Bryndrain..........................11 D2
Cae Celyn 11 D2
Cae Eithin 11 D2
Cae Grug 11 D2
Cambrian Court*, Woods Row
....12 E3
Cambrian Place 11 D3
Cambrian Way*, John St. 11 D3
Capel Dewi Road 12 G4
Capel Evan Road 12 E2
Cartref Tawelan 11 B3
Castle Hill 12 E3
Chapel Street 11 D3
Church Lane 12 E3
Church Street 12 E3
Cilddewi Park 11 A4
Cillefwr Road East 11 A5
Cillefwr Road West 11 A5
Clos Cwnin 12 F1
Clos Sticle 12 E4
Clos y Deri 12 E2
Clos y Ffynnon 12 E2
Coed y Plas..............................11 B5
College Road...................11 B2/B3
Conduit Lane............................12 E3
Coracle Way.............................12 E4
Coronation Road 11 C1
Courtlands Park 12 E2
Crispin Avenue 11 C3
Cwm Ystrad Park 11 B6
Cwmonernant 12 E1
Dan y Banc 12 E3
Dark Gate 11 D3
Derwen Fechan 11 C1
Deveraux Drive 11 D1
Dol yr Onnen.............................11 C3
Dolgwili Road 12 G1
Dyfed Close 11 B6
Elder Grove 12 F5
Elim Road 11 C1
Elliston Terrace 12 E5
Emlyn Terrace 12 F5
Esplanade, The 12 F3
Fair Lane 11 D3
Ferrar Street 11 D2
Ffynnon Waun 11 B4
Fire Station Houses 11 C2
Five Fields Path 11 C4
Fountain Hall Terrace..............11 D2
Francis Terrace 12 E3
Francis Well 12 G1
Friars House*, Friars Park Lane
....11 D3
Friars Park Lane......................11 D3

Friars Row 11 D3
Furnace Bank 12 F2
Furnace Road 12 E3
Ger y Llan 12 E3
Ger y Nant 12 F4
Glan Ffynnon...........................12 F5
Glan Tawelan 11 B4
Glan yr Ystrad 11 B6
Glannant 11 C3
Glannant Road 11 D3
Glantowy...................................12 G1
Glien Road 11 A5
Glynderi....................................12 F1
Golwg Twyi 12 F4
Gors Court 11 D3
Greenhill Close 11 D2
Greenhill*, Greenhill Close ..11 D2
Greyfriars 11 D3
Groesffordd Fach 12 E1
Grove, The 11 C2
Guildhall Square 11 D3
Hafan Tywi 12 E3
Hafod Cwnin 12 G1
Hafod Elfed 11 D2
Hall Street 12 E3
Hanover Court*, Russell Terrace
....11 D3
Haulfryn....................................12 E4
Heol Arfryn 11 A2
Heol Becca 11 B3
Heol Bolahaul 12 F6
Heol Disgwylfa 11 D2
Heol Drindod 11 B6
Heol Dyfnallt 11 D2
Heol Login 12 G5
Heol Mair 11 A2
Heol Morfa Brenin...................11 B6
Heol Rudd.................................11 C2
Heol Salem 11 B4
Heol Spurrell 11 D2
Heol y Delyn 12 E1
Heol y Wawr 11 A2
Jacksons Lane 12 E3
Jobs Well Cottages*,
      Jobs Well Road............11 B4
Jobs Well Estate 11 B3
Jobs Well Road.........................11 B3
John Street 11 D3
Jolly Tar Lane*, The Quay ...12 E4
King Street 12 E3
Knoll Gardens 11 B3
Lammas Street 11 D3
Limegrove Avenue 11 C2
Little Bridge Street*, Bridge Street
....11 D3
Little Water Street 12 E3
Llangunnor Road 12 E4
Llansteffan Road......................11 B5
Lluest yr Bryn 12 E2
Llwyn Meredith 12 E1/E2
Llygad yr Haul 12 F5
Llys Caermedi 12 F1
Llys Ffynnon 11 D2
Llys Model...............................11 B4
Llys Morfa................................12 F4
Llys y Gwehydd*, Water St. 11 D3
Llys y Nant 12 E2
Llys Ystrad 11 B5
Llysonnen Road 11 A4
Lon Hir 11 C2
Lon y Plas 11 B5
Long Acre Road 12 E2

Long Acre Villas*, Long Acre Rd.
....12 E2
Maes Dewi 11 A2
Maes Llywellyn 12 F1
Maes y Dderwen.....................11 B4
Maes y Llan 12 G4
Maes y Wennol 11 A3
Maes yr Ysgol*, St. Catherine St.
....11 D3
Manor Crescent 11 A5
Mansel Street 11 B3
Maple Crescent........................11 B3
Market Precinct*, John St. ..11 D3
Market Way...............................11 D3
Merlin Lane 11 D3
Merlin Street 11 D2
Mill Street 11 D3
Millbank Road 11 A4
Millbrook Crescent 11 C3
Monument Hill 11 B4
Morfa Lane 11 D3
Morgan Close 11 D3
Morgan Street 11 D3
Morley Street 11 D3
Mostyn Avenue........................12 G1
Mount Hill Rise 12 E5
Mount Pleasant.......................12 F5
Mount, The*, Castle Hill 12 E3
Myrddin Court 12 E3
Myrddin Crescent 12 E2
Myrtle Hill 11 D6
Nant yr Arian............................11 C2
Nash Avenue 12 G1
North Parade 12 E3
Nott Square..............................12 E3
Oak Terrace 12 F2
Oklahoma Buildings*,
      Brewery Road 11 D2
Old Grammar School*,
      The Esplanade 12 F3
Old Llangunnor Road 12 E4
Old Llansteffan Road 11 B4
Old Oak Lane 12 E2
Old Priory Road.......................12 F2
Old Station Road 12 E4
Old Stores, The*, North Parade
....12 F3
Orchard Court 12 E3
Orchard Street 12 E3
Parade Road.............................12 E3
Parade, The 12 E3
Parc Bagnall 11 D2
Parc Gwyn Estate*, Elim Road
....11 C1
Parc Thomas 11 D2
Parc y Delyn 11 D2
Parc y Ffordd 11 A4
Parc yr Afon 11 D3
Parc yr Odyn 11 A4
Parc yr Onnen 12 E1
Parcel Terrace.........................12 F2
Parcmaen Street.....................11 C3
Park Hall 12 E2/F2
Park Street 11 D3
Park Terrace 11 D3
Pen y Cae 11 A4
Penbryn Avenue 11 C3
Penlan Road 11 D1
Penlanffos Road 12 F1
Penllwyn Park 11 C3
Pensarn 12 E5
Pensarn Road..........................12 E5

Pentre Cottages 12 E3
Pentrefelin Street 11 D3
Pentremeurig Road.................11 A2
Penuel Street 12 E3
Penybanc (Pensarn) 12 E5
Penybanc (Tanerdy) 12 E5
Penymorfa.................................12 F4
Penymorfa Ganol 12 F4
Penymorfa Isaf 12 F4
Pibwrlwyd Cottages 12 E6
Pibwrlwyd Lane 12 F6
Picton Court 11 C3
Picton Place 11 C3
Picton Terrace 11 C3
Pictons Monument 11 C3
Plas Ioan 11 B6
Plas Penwern 11 B5
Plas y Ddol 11 B5
Pond Street 11 D3
Pondside 11 D3
Pondside Path 12 G2
Porth y Plas..............................11 B5
Pothouse Road 11 D3
Primrose Hill 12 F5
Priory Close.............................12 F2
Priory Row................................12 F2
Priory Street.....................12 E3/F2
Prospect Place 11 D3
Prosser Close 12 E2
Quay Street..............................11 D3
Quay Street Bank*, Quay Street
....11 D3
Quay, The 12 E4
Queen Street............................12 E3
Red Street................................11 D3
Reservoir Road 12 F1
Rhiw Babell 12 E1
Rhodfa Glyndwr 12 E1
Rhos Las 12 F4
Richmond Close 12 E2
Richmond Cottages 12 E2
Richmond Court*, Richmond Ter.
....12 E2
Richmond Terrace 12 E2
Roman Road.............................12 E5
Ropewalk 12 F2
Rose Terace 11 C3
Ross Avenue 12 F1/F2
Royal Oak Cottages 11 B4
Royal Oak Terrace 11 B4
Russell Terrace........................11 C2
Seymour Terrace 12 E2
Southern Terrace 12 E4
Spilman Street 12 E3
Spring Gardens 11 D4
Springfield Road 12 E2
St. Andrews Road....................12 E3
St. Catherine Street 11 D3
St. Clears Road 11 D3
St. Davids Avenue 11 C3
St. Davids Place*, Lammas St.
....11 D3
St. Davids Street.....................11 D3
St. Johns Court 12 E3
St. Mary Street 12 E3
St. Nons Avenue......................11 C3
St. Peters Court 12 E3
St. Peters Street 12 E3
Station Approach 12 E4
Steele Avenue 11 C3
Stephens Way 11 D5
Sticle Path 12 E4/E5

Swans Lane 11 D3
Sycamore Way 11 B3
Tabernacle Terrace 11 D2
Tanerdy 12 F1
Temple Gardens*, Mansel Street
...........................11 D3
Tir Ysgawen 12 F4/F5
Towy Close 11 B6
Towy Mews*, Priory Street ..12 F2
Towy Side 12 E3
Towy View 12 F2
Trefechan Road 11 A2
Tregynwr 12 F5
Trem y Bedol................12 F2
Trem y Coleg 11 B2
Trem y Dref.................12 F2
Trevaughan Road.............11 C1
Troedybryn*, Jobs Well Rd...11 B4
Ty Coch Cottages............11 D6
Ty Hir 11 C3
Ty Rhys.....................12 E3
Tygwyn Court 11 B4
Under Parade Road 12 E3
Union Street 11 C3
Victoria Place 11 D5
Water Street 11 D3
Waterloo Terrace 11 D2
Waun Iago 11 B3
Waun Meadows 11 B3
Weavers Court*, Water Street
...........................11 D3
Wellfield Road 11 D2
Winsora 12 G4
Woodbine Cottages 11 B4
Woods Row 12 E3
Y Garreg Filltir*, Abbey Mead
...........................12 F2
Y Talar.....................12 F5
Yr Aelwydd 12 F5
Ystrad Close 11 B4
Ystrad Drive 11 B6

CROSS HANDS, CEFNEITHIN & GORSLAS

Acer Court 20 G5
Bancyffynnon 20 G2
Bellvue 20 F4
Black Lion Road 20 F4
Brookfield Terrace 20 E4
Bryndewi 20 E4
Brynlluan 20 E4
Caeglas 20 G3
Carmarthen Road 20 F1
Cefneithin Road 20 E3
Church Road.................20 E4
Clos Emily..................20 G5
Clos Pen y Waun 20 G5
Clos Trefenty...............20 E1
Clos y Waun 20 G3
Crescent, The 20 F5
Crosshands Road 20 F4
Cwm Mwyn 20 F4
Dobel Terrace 20 E5
Ffordd y Morfa 20 G6
Garreg Hollt................20 F2
Gate Road...................20 E6
Glaspant 20 E5
Gors Ddu Road 20 G6
Gors Ddu Terrace............20 G6
Grove Hill 20 E5

Grove Hill Park 20 F5
Heol Bryngwili 20 H1
Heol Derwen 20 G5
Heol Las 20 F3
Heol Parc Mawr 20 G4/H4
Heol Rhos Bowen 20 E1
Heol Stanllyd 20 G3
Heol Trefenty 20 F1
Heol y Dre 20 F2
Heol y Foel 20 E1
Heol y Parc 20 E1
Heol yr Ysgol 20 E1/E2
Llandeilo Road 20 G3
Llys Eithin 20 E5
Maes Derwen 20 G5
Maes yr Haf 20 H2
Maesgors 20 G6
Meadows Road...............20 G3/H4
Norman Terrace 20 E5
Norton Road 20 F5
Parc Menter 20 H5
Penygroes Road 20 E4
Pontardulais Road 20 G3
Poplar Court 20 G3
Thornhill Road 20 H6
Tirwaun 20 H3
Ty Newydd Terrace 20 G4
Woodlands Terrace 20 H3
Y Fron 20 F1
Y Glyn 20 E1

DREFACH

Bron yr Ynn 28 G2
Brynglas 28 F2
Brynheulog 28 F3
Brynhyfryd..................28 E2
Cae Ffynon 28 F1
Cae Gwyn 28 F1
Cwm Mawr Lodge 28 G2
Dyffryn Villas 28 F2
Gwynfryn 28 F2
Hen Ffordd 28 G2
Heol Afallon 28 G2
Heol Blaenhirwaun 28 G2
Heol Capel Sion 28 G2
Heol Cwm Bach 28 G3
Heol Cwmmawr 28 G2
Heol Ddu 28 F2
Heol Ty Isaf 28 E2
Llys Seion 28 E2
Mary Street 28 G3
Nant y Dderwen 28 F2
Uwchgwendraeth 28 G3
Woodlands Terrace...........28 F2
Yr Hafan 28 F2

FERRYSIDE

Arch, The 35 C5
Beach Cottages 35 C5
Brigstocke Terrace 35 C5
Caradoc Court 35 C5
Carmarthen Road 35 D4/D6
Cliff, The 35 C6
Coast Road 35 C6
Coburg Villas 35 C5
Eva Terrace 35 C4
Glan Tywi 35 D4/D6
Glan yr Ystrad 35 D6
Glanmorfa...................35 D6
Glantywi Uchaf 35 C5
Hall Terrace 35 C5
Holcwm Way..................35 C6

Llys Holcwm 35 C6
Maesyffynon 35 D4
Manselton Villas 35 C5
Mount Pleasant..............35 D4
Pale Cottages 35 D4
Port Way 35 D5
Portway Cottages 35 C5
Tripenhead Road 35 D5
Vicarage Close 35 D4
Water Street 35 C4
Wellfield Terrace 35 D4

FISHGUARD & GOODWICK ABERGWAUN & WDIG

Allt y Carne 21 C1
Anthorn 21 D5
Back Lane 21 D1
Bank Terrace 21 C5
Bridge Cottages 21 B3
Bridge Street 21 C5
Brodog Court 21 C4
Brodog Lane 21 C4
Brodog Terrace 21 C4
Bryn Awelon 21 A1
Bryn Elfed 21 B4
Bryn Gomer 21 A4
Bryn Llewellyn 21 D5
Bryn Road 21 C4
Bryn Siriol 21 D5
Brynteg 21 A2
Cae Gerddi 21 A1
Carreg Onnen 21 D4
Church Terrace 21 B1
Clement Road 21 A2
Clive Road 21 C3
Clos y Bigney 21 D3
Clos y Gongol 21 D4
Coronation Road 21 C4
Cross Street 21 B2
Dan y Bryn 21 D5
Drim Terrace 21 B1
Emlyn Terrace 21 C1
Erw Las 21 C4
Feidr Castell 21 D4
Feidr Dylan 21 B4
Feidr Fraich 21 D4
Feidr Gongol 21 D4
Feidr Pen Commins 21 C3
French Walk 21 B3
Garn Fawr 21 D4
Garn Ingli 21 D5
Garn Winda 21 D4
Garnlas 21 D5
Gasworks Hill 21 B3
Glan y Mor Road 21 B1
Glyn y Mel Road 21 D5
Goedwig Terrace 21 B2
Goedwig Villas 21 B2
Goodwick Hill 21 B1
Gwaun View 21 D5
Gwelfor 21 D4
Hamilton Street 21 C4
Haverfordwest Road 21 D3
Heol Caradog 21 D5
Heol Cerwyn 21 D4
Heol Cleddau 21 D4
Heol Crwys 21 B4
Heol Dewi 21 B3

Heol Dyfed 21 C3
Heol Emrys 21 C4
Heol Glyndwr 21 D5
Heol Penlan 21 A1
Heol Preseli 21 D4
Heol Trefin 21 B4
Heol y Felin 21 C1
High Street 21 D4
Hill Street 21 A1
Hill Terrace 21 C5
Hillside Close 21 C1
Hillside Crescent 21 C1
Hillside Home 21 C1
Hottipass Street 21 D5
Jacksons Way 21 B1
Jubilee Terrace 21 C1
Kensington Street (Fishguard)
...........................21 C5
Kensington Street (Goodwick)
...........................21 B1
Lampit Way 21 C5
Llain Las 21 D5
Llanychaer Road 21 D5
Llys Onnen 21 C1
Lota Park Road..............21 D4
Maes yr Afon*, Manor Way..21 B2
Maesgruig 21 C1
Maesgwyn Road 21 D1/D3
Main Street (Fishguard) 21 C5
Main Street (Goodwick) 21 B2
Manor Parade 21 B1
Manor Way 21 B1
Marchgate Paddock 21 C4
Marine Walk 21 B4
Market Square 21 C4
Morfa Las 21 B1
Nant y Ffynnon 21 B1
New Hill Road 21 A2
New Hill Villas 21 A2
New Road 21 B2
Newport Road 21 C6
Old Newport Road 21 C6
Oxford House 21 A1
Pant yr Chain 21 A2
Pant yr Chain Cottages......21 A2
Pantycelyn 21 B4
Parc y Shwt.................21 D4
Park Loktudi 21 D5
Park Sreet (Goodwick) 21 A1
Park Street (Fishguard) 21 D5
Parrog, The 21 B3
Pen Banc 21 D4
Pen Wallis 21 D5
Pen y Bryn 21 C3
Penslade 21 C4
Penslade Terrace 21 C4
Plas y Gamil Road 21 B1
Prescelly Crescent 21 A1
Quay Road (Fishguard)......21 C5
Quay Road (Goodwick) 21 A2
Railway Terrace 21 B1
Rewey Terrace 21 B1
Ropeyard 21 C4
Ropeyard Close 21 D3
Ropeyard Lane 21 D3
Seaview Crescent 21 B1
Siriole 21 A2
Slade Cottages 21 C5
Slade, The 21 C5
Sladeway 21 C4
Smyth Street 21 C5
St. Davids Place 21 B2

Station Hill.....

Station Hill	21 A2
Terminal Road	21 A2
Tlysfan	21 D5
Tower Hill	21 C5
Trem y Mor	21 C3
Troed y Rhiw	21 C1
Vergam Terrace	21 C4
Victoria Avenue	21 C4
Victoria House	21 C4
Wallis Crescent	21 D5
Wallis Street	21 D5
Wern Road	21 B2
West Street	21 C4
Windy Hall	21 B3
Y Ganol*, High Street	21 D4
Y Gorlan*, Main Street	21 B2

GLANAMAN & GARNANT

Arcade Terrace	22 G4
Bishop Road	22 G5
Bro Ryan	22 G2
Bryn Lloi Road	22 F2
Bryncethin Road	22 G6
Ceidrim Road	22 G4
Church Row	22 G5
Clos Felin	22 F4
Coronation Road	22 G5
Cowell Road	22 H6
Cwmamman Road	22 G1
Cwrt Tomos	22 G6
Dan y Deri	22 F2
Deri Road	22 G1
Dynevor Road	22 G5
Folland Road	22 F2
Ger yr Afon	22 F2
Glanffrwd Villas	22 G4
Glyn Powell	22 F1
Greenfield Road	22 G5
Grenig Road	22 G2
Hendre Road	22 F5
Heol Amman	22 F1
Heol Felin	22 E4
High Street	22 F3
Highfield Road	22 F5
Jolly Road	22 G6
Jones Terrace	22 G1
Llandeilo Road	22 E4
Llwyncelyn Road	22 G1
Llys Sant Margaret	22 F2
Lon Llwyd	22 F4
Lon y Derwydd	22 G6
Lower Station Road	22 G5
Maes y Fron	22 G4
Maesgrenig	22 G1
Maesybedol	22 F5
Maesybont	22 F1
Maesyglyn	22 F1
Maesyhendre	22 F4
Maesywern Road	22 G1
Mountain Road	22 E1
Nant Gwineu Road	22 G6
Nantyglyn Road	22 F1
Neuadd Road	22 G6
New Ceidrim Road	22 G4
New School Road	22 G4
Oakfield Road	22 F5
Parc Bryn Rhos	22 G2
Parc Glan yr Afon	22 F4
Parc Glanffrwd	22 G4
Penpound Lane	22 F1
Penyrallt	22 H6
Rhodfa Bryn Rhos	22 G2
Station Road	22 F2
Stepney Road	22 G6
Tabernacle Road	22 F1
Tan y Gelli	22 F6
Tir Syr Walter	22 F6
Tir y Coed Road	22 E2
Tyle Glas	22 H6
Upper Station Road	22 G5
Vicarage Road	22 G5
Waunhwyad Lane	22 E2
Wern Road	22 G4

HAVERFORDWEST HWLFFORDD

Abbots Close	14 F4
Addison Close	14 E5
Albany Court*, Rose Lane	14 E4
Albany Terrace	14 E4
Albert Street	14 E3
Augustine Way	14 F3
Avallenau Home	14 G3
Back Lane	13 C5
Bank Row	14 E4
Baring Gould Close	13 D3
Baring Gould Way	13 D3
Barn Court	14 E4
Barn Street	14 E3
Beech Tree Gardens	14 F4
Beechlands Park	14 F2
Bethany Road	14 F1
Bethany Row	13 D6
Bridge Street	13 D4
Bridgend Square	13 D5
Brooklands Park	14 F2
Brooks Grove Lane	14 G1
Bush Row	14 E4
Byron Road	14 F5
Cambrian Place	14 E5
Caradoc Place	14 E2
Caradogs Well Road	14 G2
Cardigan Road	13 B6/C5
Cartlett	13 D5
Cartlett Road	13 D5
Cashfield Way	13 B3
Castle Back	13 D4
Castle High	13 D4
Castle Hill*, Castle Back	13 D4
Castle Square	13 D4
Castle Street	13 D4
Castle Terrace	13 D4
Castle View	13 D4
Catherines Gate	14 H4
Cawdor Close	14 F2
Century Close	13 B4
Chapel Lane	13 D4
Cherry Grove	13 D5
Church Lane (Centre)	14 E4
Church Lane (Prendergast)	13 C5
Church Street	13 D4
City Road	13 D3
Clareston Close	13 D3
Clay Lane	14 F5/G4
Cleddau Avenue	14 E5
Clover Park	14 E6
College Court	14 E4
Coronation Avenue	13 C5
Court Road	13 D2
Creamstone Road	14 E6
Cromie Avenue	14 E3
Cromwell Court*, Spring Gardens	13 D4
Crowhill Road	13 A3
Cuffern Close	13 D3
Curlew Close	13 D2
Daffodil Drive	13 B4
Dale Road	14 E2/F1
Dark Street	13 D4
Deans Close	14 F3
Delapoer Drive	14 F2
Dew Street	14 E4
Douglas James Close	14 E1
Douglas James Way	13 D1
Dredgman Hill	14 H2
Dunsany Park	14 E6
Ebenezer Row	13 D4
Ellis Avenue	14 E4
Fair Oakes	14 F2
Falcon Road	13 D2
Fenton Court	14 E3
Fern Hill Lane	14 G5
Fern Hill Road	14 G4
Ferry Way	14 H4
Fir Tree Close	14 G3
Fishguard Road	13 C5
Fleming Crescent	13 D3
Foley Way	14 E4
Fortunes Frolic	14 E6/F6
Fountain Row	14 E2
Freemens View	14 G4
Freemens Way	14 E5/F4
Friars Lane, The	13 D4
Furzy Park	14 E1
Gerald Road	14 E2
Glebe House	14 E4
Glen View	14 G3
Glenafon View	13 B5
Glenfields Road	14 G2
Glenover Cottages	14 F2
Glenover Park	14 E1
Gloucester Terrace*, Holloway	13 D4
Goat Street	14 E4
Goldcrest Avenue	14 E1
Goshawk Road	13 D2
Greenfield Close	13 C5
Greenhill Crescent	14 G4/H4
Greenhill Park Drive	14 H4
Guillemot Avenue	13 B4
Hammond Avenue	14 F4
Hanover Court	14 E3
Haroldston Close	14 G4
Haroldston Lane	14 E4
Haroldston Terrace	14 F3
Harrier Road	13 D2
Haven Park Avenue	14 E1
Haven Park Close	14 E1
Haven Park Crescent	14 E1
Haven Park Drive	14 E1
Haven Road	14 E1
Hawthorn Rise	14 E1
Hayguard Lane	13 D4
Haylett Lane	14 G3/H3
Heol Derwen	14 G4
Heritage Park	13 B6
Hermitage Grove	13 B5
Hermons Hill	14 E4
High Street	14 E4
Highgrove	14 E1
Highlands Avenue	13 D3
Hill Street	14 E4
Hole in the Wall	13 D4
Holloway	13 D4
Horns Lane	14 E4
Horse Fair	14 F3
Howells Avenue	14 E2
Hywel Road	14 E2
Jenkins Close	14 G4
Jockey Fields	14 C5
Jury Lane	14 E2
Keats Grove	14 F5
Kestrel Road	14 E1
Kiln Road*, North Street	13 D4
Kingsmere Close	13 B5
Laburnum Grove	14 F4
Laurel Drive	14 F2
Lexton Terrace	14 E4
Lindsway Park	13 B6
Longfellow Close	14 F5
Lynnefield	14 G3
Magdalen Street	14 G3
Maple Avenue	14 F2
Mariners Square	13 D4
Market Street	14 E4
Marychurch Court*, Albert Street	14 E3
Masefield Drive	14 F5
Mayoral Terrace	13 C5
Meadow View	13 C4
Merlins Avenue	14 G3
Merlins Court	14 E4
Merlins Crest	14 F3
Merlins Hill	14 F3
Merlins Terrace	14 F3
Milford Road	13 D5
Mill Bank	13 D5
Mill Lane	14 G3
Mill Road	13 D5
Milton Close	14 F5
Milward Close	13 D4
Moravian Court*, Market Street	14 E4
Morgan Terrace	14 E4
Narberth Road	13 D4
Nelson Villas	14 E4
Nether Edge Drive	14 F3
New Crown Buildings	14 E4
New Road	14 E4
North Court	13 D4
North Crescent	13 D4
North Gate	13 D4
North Street	13 D4
Nubian Avenue	14 E4
Oakwood Grove	13 C3
Old Bridge	13 D4
Old Bridge Relief Road	13 D4
Old Hakin Road	14 H4
Osprey Drive	13 D2
Palmerston Road	14 F4
Park Corner Road	14 F4
Park Road	13 D4
Park Villa Court	13 C4
Pembroke Road	14 G5
Penns Close	14 F2
Percy Terrace	14 E4
Peregrine Close	13 D2
Perrot Avenue	13 D3
Perrots Road	13 D4
Picton Place	13 D4
Police Houses	14 F4
Portfield	14 E4
Portfield Avenue	14 E4
Poyston Close	13 D2
Prendergast	13 D4

Prescelly Park 13 B5
Prescelly Road 13 D3
Primrose Drive 13 B4
Princess Royal Way 14 E4
Priory Avenue 14 F4
Priory Courts 14 E5
Priory Mill Cottages 14 F5
Prospect Place 13 D5
Pyx Parade*, Perrots Rd. 13 D4
Quay Street.........................14 E4
Queen Square 13 D4
Queens Ditch 13 D3
Queensway..........................13 D5
Rackhill Court 13 D3
Rackhill Terrace 13 D3
Redhill Park 13 C4
Richmond Crescent 14 E3
Rifleman Lane.....................14 E4
Rise, The 13 D5
Riverside Arcade*,
  The Friars Lane...........13 D4
Rose Avenue 14 G4
Rosemary Lane 14 E4
Ruther Park 14 E1
Salutation Square 13 D5
Sanderling Close 13 D2
Scarrowscant Lane 14 F2/F3
Scotchwell Lane 13 C5/C6
Scotchwell View 13 C5
Scotchwell Walk 13 D5
Shakespeare Close............14 F4
Shelley Road.......................14 F4
Shipmans Lane...................14 E4
Shoals Hook Lane 13 C6
Shoemakers Court*, Market St.
  ....14 E4
Signal Way 13 B3
Siskin Close 13 D2
Skinners Lane.....................13 D4
Slade Lane 13 C2
Slade Park 13 C4
Slade Villas 13 C2
Snowdrop Close 14 F1
Snowdrop Lane...................14 E2
South Court.........................13 D1
Spenser Way.......................14 F5
Spring Gardens Lane 13 D4
Springfield Close.................13 B5
St. Anthonys Way 14 F3
St. Davids Road 13 B1
St. Issells Avenue...............14 G4
St. Margarets Close 14 G4
St. Marks Close 14 G3
St. Martins Park 13 C4
St. Marys Street*, Tower Hill
  ....14 E4
St. Thomas Avenue 14 G4
St. Thomas Green 14 E4
Stepney Terrace 13 C5
Stokes Avenue 13 C5
Style Park 14 E6
Swan Square 13 D4
Sycamore Flats*, St. Issells Av.
  ....14 G4
Sydney Rees Way 13 C5
Tan Bank 13 C5
Taylor Apartments*, North Street
  ....13 D4
Thomas Parry Way.............13 D3
Tower Hill 14 E4
Trafalgar Close 14 E4
Trafalgar Road 13 D2

Trevaughan Close 14 E4
Tudor Gardens 14 G4/H4
Tudor Way 14 E2
Under the Hills 14 G2
Union Hill.............................14 E5
Upper Market Street 14 E4
Uzmaston Road 14 E6
Vawers Close 13 D3
Venns Close 14 G4
Victoria Place 13 D4
Walters Avenue 14 G4
Well Lane 13 C5
West Court 13 D1
Williamston Close 14 E2
Winch Crescent 14 E4
Winch Lane 14 E4
Windsor Way.......................14 E5
Withybush Road 13 A5/B5
Woodlands Park 14 G3
Wordsworth Avenue 14 F5

KILGETTY

Alma Cottages.....................36 F2
Ash Park 36 F2
Begelly Cross 36 E2
Carmarthen Road 36 E2
Cotswold Gardens 36 E2
Heritage Gardens 36 F2
Ivy Chimney Lane 36 F3
James Park 36 E2
Kerrs Way 36 F1
Kilgetty Cottages 36 F2
Kilvelgy Park 36 F2
Mayfield...............................36 F2
Mayfield Acres.....................36 F2
New Road 36 E2
Newton Terrace 36 F2
Oakfield Court*, Oakfield Drive
  ....36 F2
Oakfield Drive 36 F2
Park Avenue 36 F2
Ryelands Lane 36 E1
Ryelands Place 36 F1
Ryelands Way 36 F1
Shillingford Park 36 F2
St. Marys Place 36 F2
Station Road 36 F2
Woodland Avenue 36 F1

LAMPETER
LLANBEDR
PONT STEFFAN

Aberaeron Road 28 F4
Bangor Court.......................28 F5
Barley Mow 28 F6
Bridge Street.......................28 G6
Bryn Hebog 28 F5
Bryn Road 28 F5
Bryn Steffan 28 F4
Bryn yr Eglwys 28 F5
Cae Dash 28 F6
Cambrian Road 28 F5
Cellan Road 28 H6
Church Street 28 F5
College Street 28 F5
Common, The 28 F6
Drovers Road 28 F6
Falcondale Drive.................28 E4
Ffynnonbedr 28 F5
Forest Road 28 F4
Glandulais Terrace 28 G5

Glyndwr*, Station Terrace ..28 G5
Greenfield Terrace 28 F6
Gwel y Creddyn 28 F4
Harford Row 28 F6
Harford Square 28 F5
High Street 28 F5
Kingsmead 28 F6
Llanfair Road 28 G6
Llanwen Road 28 E6
Llys Deri 28 F5
Llys Pedr 28 F5
Llys Teifi 28 G6
Maes y Deri 28 F4
Maestir Road.......................28 E5
Maesycoed 28 F4
Maesyfelin 28 F5
Maesyllan 28 F5
Market Street.......................28 F5
Mill Street 28 F5
Mount Walk 28 F5
New Street 28 F6
North Road 28 F4
Parc y Felin 28 G4
Pen Bryn 28 F4
Peterwell Terrace 28 F5
Picton Lane 28 F6
Pleasant Hill Cottages........28 F4
Pontfaen Road 28 E5
Royal Oak Mews*, Market Street
  ....28 F5
St. Thomas Street 28 F5
Station Terrace 28 G5
Taliesen Court 28 G6
Teifi Terrace 28 F6
Temple Terrace 28 F5
Tregaron Road 28 F4
Victoria Terrace...................28 F6

LAUGHARNE
LACHARN

Back Lane 36 G3
Butts, The 36 G2
Castle Cottages 36 H2
Church Street 36 G1
Cliff Road 36 H2
Clifton Street 36 H1
Clyde Cottages....................36 G1
Cwrt Woodford 36 G3
Duncan Street.....................36 G2
Dylan Lodges 36 H1
Dylans Walk 36 H2
Edina Dails Park 36 G1
Ferrys Chalets 36 H2
Fountain Row 36 H2
Frogmore Gardens 36 G3
Frogmore Street 36 G2
Glen Road...........................36 H1
Gosport Street 36 G3
Grist Square*, The Grist 36 G2
Grist, The 36 G2
Holloway Road 36 G2
Horsepool Road 36 G1
King Street 36 H2
Kington Gardens 36 H2
Laques, The 36 G2
Mackrel Lake 36 G3
Market Lane 36 H1
Market Street 36 H2
Milford Chalets 36 H3
Moir Gardens 36 G2
Newbridge Road..................36 G2

Orchard Park 36 G3
Pembroke Lodges 36 H1
St. Davids Chalets 36 H2
Stoneway Road 36 G3
Strand Cottages 36 H3
Strand, The 36 H2
Upton House........................36 H1
Victoria Street 36 H1
Water Street 36 G2
Wogan Mews 36 G2
Wogan Street 36 H2

LLANDEILO

Abbey Terrace 29 C3
Abernant Cottages 29 A1
Alan Road 29 C2
Bank Buildings 29 C2
Bank Terrace 29 B3
Bethlehem Road..................29 D3
Blende Road 29 C2
Bridge Street 29 B3
Bro Hywel 29 B2
Brooklands Terrace 29 C1
Brynawel Terrace 29 B2
Carmarthen Road 29 A1
Carmarthen Street 29 B2
Church Street 29 B3
Cilcennen Terrace 29 C1
Clarence Road 29 C2
Clarendon Road 29 C2
Clos Garth Madryn 29 B2
Crescent Road 29 C2
Diana Road 29 C2
Dirleton Terrace 29 C2
Dynevor Avenue 29 B2
Garreg Las 29 C2
George Hill 29 B3
George Street 29 B3
Greenfield Place 29 B2
Heol y Garreglas.................29 C2
King Street 29 B3
Latimer Road 29 C2
Lewis Terrace 29 C2
Llandeilo Bypass.................29 A1
Llys Pengrug 29 B2
Lon Caeffynnon 29 B2
Lon Rhys 29 B1/B2
Maes Elfryn 29 B2
Maes y Farchnad 29 C2
Maes y Glyn 29 B2
Market Street 29 B3
Mews, The*, Rhosmaen Street
  ....29 C2
New Road 29 B2
North Bank 29 B2
Orchard Place 29 B2
Parc Lewis 29 B2
Parc Pengrug 29 B1
Quay Street.........................29 B3
Railway Terrace 29 C2
Rhosmaen Street 29 C2
St. Pauls Court 29 C2
Station Road 29 C1
Stepney Road 29 C1
Talley Road.........................29 C1
Thomas Street 29 C2
Thomas Terrace 29 C2
Wellfield Terrace 29 B2
Whitfield Terrace 29 B2
Y Trallwng 29 C1
Yr Hafod 29 B2
Ysgubor Abad 29 C3

LLANDOVERY LLANYMDDYFRI

Adelaide Street 29 C5
Brecon Road 29 D5
Bridge Street 29 C6
Broad Street 29 B6
Castle Street 29 C6
Church Bank 29 B6
Cilycwm Road 29 B4
College View 29 B5
Dan y Crug 29 D5
Dingat Close 29 B5
Dingat Terrace 29 B6
Dolau Bran 29 C5
Garden Lane 29 B6
Gasworks Lane 29 B6
Gelli Deg 29 C5
Heol Pluguffan 29 B6
Heol Rhos 29 A4
Heol Royston 29 C6
High Street 29 C6
Kings Road 29 B6
Llandeilo Road 29 A5
Llanfair Hill 29 C4
Llanfair Road 29 B4
Llys Llanfair 29 B4
Lon Rhys Pritchard 29 B6
Lower Road 29 B6
Maes y Coleg 29 B5
Maesglas 29 B5
Market Square 29 B6
New Road 29 B5
Orchard Street 29 C5
Picton Court 29 D6
Queen Street 29 C5
Queensway 29 B5
Railway Terrace 29 B5
Rock Cottages 29 B6
School Lane 29 B5
Stone Street 29 B5
Tywi Avenue 29 B5
Victoria Crescent 29 B5
Victoria Street 29 C5
Water Street 29 C5

LLANDYBIE

Ammanford Road 30 F1
Blaenau Road 30 F2/F3
Caecoed 30 F2/F3
Caeffynnon Road 30 G1
Caergroes 30 F2
Campbell Road 30 G1
Church Street 30 F1
Derwen Fawr 30 G3
Ffordd y Blodau 30 G3
Gelly Road 30 F2
Glynhir Road 30 G3
Heol Ceirios 30 G3
Heol Gwilym 30 F1
Heol Marlais 30 F2
High Street 30 F1
Kings Road 30 G1
Llandeilo Road 30 F1
Llys y Nant 30 F1
Maes yr Helyg........................ 30 G3
Maespiode 30 F2
Maidens Grove 30 G2
Margaret Road 30 F2
McKays Road 30 G3
Parc y Llan 30 F1
Plas Lan 30 F1
Rawlings Road 30 F2
Tan y Lan 30 G3
Waunfarlais Road.................. 30 G3
Woodfield Avenue 30 F2
Woodfield Road 30 F2

LLANDYSUL

Alma, The 37 C6
Barley Mow 37 C5
Beeches, The 37 C4/C5
Bridge Street 37 C6
Cambrian Terrace.................. 37 D5
Chapel Street 37 C6
Charles Street 37 C5
Church Street 37 C5/D4
Cilgwyn Row*, Lincoln St......37 C6
Clifton Terrace 37 C5
Council Bungalows*, Lincoln St.
.... 37 C6
Cysgod y Llan 37 D5
Glascoed 37 C5
Graig Road 37 C4/C5
Green Hill 37 C5
Heol y Gilfach 37 B5
Heol y Neuadd 37 C5
High Street 37 C5
King Street 37 C5
Lewis Street 37 B6
Lincoln Street 37 C6
Llyn y Fran 37 B4
Llys y Wawr 37 C5
Lon Channing 37 C5
Lon Fedwen 37 C5
Lon Letty 37 C5
Marble Terrace 37 C5
Morris Terrace 37 C6
New Road 37 C6
Parc yr Ynn 37 B4
Pencader Road 37 C6
Pentrecourt Road 37 A6
Plygyrhiw................................ 37 D5
Porth Terrace 37 C5
Seion Hill 37 C5
Spring Croft*, Lon Letty 37 C5
Spring Gardens 37 C5
Station Road 37 C6
Station Yard 37 C6
Trem y Teifi 37 C5
Ty Bad Gardens 37 D5
Union Flats*, Church St. 37 C5
Well Street 37 C5
Wesley Lane 37 C5
Wilks Head Square................ 37 C6
Wind Street 37 C6

LLANGADOG

Bryniago 36 F5
Castle Close 36 E5
Church Street 36 E4
Glandyrfal 36 F5
Golwg y Mynydd 36 F5
Gurrey Cottages*, Walters Road
.... 36 E4
Heol Pendref 36 F5
High Street 36 F5
Penygraig Villas 36 F5
Rhyd y Fro.............................. 36 F4
Station Road 36 E4
Trehelig 36 E4
Vicarage Road 36 E4
Walters Road 36 E4
Bethel Row 36 H4

LLANSTEFFAN

Bethel Terrace 36 H5
Brondeg Cottages 36 G5
Brook Cottages...................... 36 G5
Bryn House 36 H4
Church Road.......................... 36 H5
Eglwys Ger Yr 36 H5
Glan y Mor 36 H5
High Street 36 H5
Innisfree Cottages 36 H5
Ivy Cottages 36 G5
Maes Griffith 36 H5
Mill,The 36 H4
New Cottages 36 G5
Old Road 36 G5
Old School Road 36 H4
Stratford Cottages 36 H5
Stratford Villas 36 H5
Water Lane 36 H5

MILFORD HAVEN ABERDAUGHLEDDAU

Albion Street 16 E4
Ardent Close 16 G3
Ash Grove.............................. 16 G4
Barlow Street 16 E5
Bay View Drive 15 C5
Beach Hill 16 G4
Birch Mead 16 G4
Blackbridge 16 H5
Blackbridge Crescent............ 16 H5
Blackbridge Drive 16 H5
Brick Houses 16 G6
Bridge Street 15 D5
Brooke Avenue 16 F5
Bunkers Hill 16 G3
Caldy Way 16 F3
Camuset Close 15 C4
Castle Hall Drive 16 H5
Castle Hall Road 16 G5
Castle Pill Crescent 16 H2
Castle Pill Road 16 H2
Castle Terrace........................ 16 F4
Cedar Court 15 D4
Cellar Hill 16 G5
Central Court.......................... 16 F4
Chapel Street 16 E6
Charles Street 16 E5
Cherry Tree Close 16 G4
Chestnut Way 16 G4
Church Road.......................... 15 C4
Clay Lane 15 B4
Concrete Houses 16 G6
Conduit Lane 15 D6
Conway Drive 16 H2
Coombs Drive 16 F4
Coombs Road 16 G4
Court Rise 15 C4
Croft Avenue 15 B5
Cromwell Road 16 E2
Cutty Sark Drive 16 G3
Dairy Park 15 D5
Dale Road 15 A2
Dartmouth Gardens 16 E5
Dartmouth Street 16 E5
Derwent Avenue 16 H2
Dewsland Street 16 E5
Docks, The 16 E5
Eastleigh Drive 16 F5
Edward Street 16 E5
Elizabeth Venmore Court 16 F5
Elm Lane 16 G4
Exeter Road 16 H2
Fairsea Close 15 B5
Fishermans Walk 16 E1
Fold, The 16 E1
Fort Rise 15 C6
Francis Street 16 F5
Fulke Street............................ 16 E5
Gateholm Avenue.................. 16 G4
Gelliswick Road...................... 15 B6/C5
George Street 16 E4
Glastonbury House 16 F3
Glebelands 15 C5
Gorsewood Drive 15 C6
Grassholm Close 16 F3
Great North Road 16 F5
Green Close 16 G2
Green Terrace 15 C4
Greville Road 16 F5
Grove Housing Estate 16 H3
Gwili Road 15 D5
Hakin Point............................ 15 D6
Hakin Ville.............................. 15 D6
Hamilton Terrace 16 E5
Harbour Way 15 C5
Haven Drive 15 B4
Haven Heights*, Robert St. 16 E5
Hawthorn Path 16 G4
Hayston Avenue 15 D6
Hill Street 15 D5
Hilton Avenue 16 G4
Howarth Close 16 E3
Hubberton Road 16 F5
Imogen Place 16 F5
Imperial Terrace 16 F4
James Street.......................... 15 D5
John Lewis Street 15 B5
Jordans Close........................ 16 H2
Larch Road 16 G4
Lawrence Cottages................ 15 D4
Liddeston Close 15 C3
Liddeston Valley 15 C4
Lilac Close.............................. 16 G3
Linney Way 16 F3
Lower Thornton Road............ 16 E1
Lundy Close 16 F3
Mable Hall Close 16 F4
Mable Hall Road 16 F3
Manchester Square................ 16 F5
Mansfield Street 16 F5
Marine Boulevard 16 E5
Marine Gardens 16 E5
Mariners Way 16 H2
Market Square 16 E4
Meads Court 16 E4
Meyler Crescent 16 F3
Milford Road 16 H1
Milton Crescent 16 G5
Milton House.......................... 16 G5
Monnow Close 16 H2
Moorcroft Road...................... 15 C5
Mount Pleasant Way 16 G3
Murray Road 16 G6
Nelson Avenue 15 D5
Neyland Road (Coombs) 16 H5
Neyland Road (Steynton) 16 H1
Nubian Crescent.................... 15 D6
Oaklands 16 G4
Oberon Grove........................ 16 G2
Observatory Avenue.............. 15 C5
Phillips Avenue 16 F4

Picton Close 15 C5
Picton Road 15 C5/C6
Pier Road 16 F6
Pill Fold 16 G5
Pill Lane......16 F5
Pill Road 16 F4
Point Street 15 D5/16 E6
Pointfields Crescent 15 D6
Pond Meadow......16 H2
Prescelly Court*,
  Slaughterhouse La.......16 E5
Prescelly Place 16 E4
Priory Court 16 F4
Priory Hill 16 E3
Priory Lodge Close 16 E4
Priory Lodge Drive 16 E4
Priory Road......16 E5
Priory Street 16 E5
Priory Vale Approach*,
  Murray Road 16 F4
Prioryville......16 F4
Ramsey Drive 16 F3
Rath, The 16 F6
Rectory Avenue 15 C5
Richard John Road 16 F4
Richmond Terrace 16 F5
Robert Street......16 E5
Roebuck Close 16 H2
Romilly Crescent......15 D4
Rope Walk, The 15 D5
Sandhurst Road 16 F6
Shakespeare Avenue 16 F5
Sheffield Drive 16 H2
Silverstream......15 C4
Silverstream Crescent 15 D4
Silverstream Drive 15 C4
Skomer Drive 16 F2/F3
Slaughterhouse Lane 16 E5
Slip Hill 16 F5
South Hook Road 15 A6
Spikes Lane 15 D5
St. Annes Drive......15 D6
St. Annes Place 15 D5
St. Annes Road 15 D5
St. Brides Way 16 F3
St. Davids Park 15 C4
St. Davids Road 16 E4
St. Lawrence Avenue 15 D5
St. Lawrence Close 15 D5
St. Lawrence Hill......15 C4
St. Peters Road......16 E5
Starbuck Road 16 E4
Stephen Street 16 E5
Steynton Road 16 F4
Stone Court......16 F4
Stratford House 16 F5
Stratford Road......16 E5
Sycamore Close 16 G4
Thornton Housing Estate 16 G2
Thornton Road 16 F2
Tollgate Court 16 F4
Trafalgar Road 16 E5
Trinity Place 16 E5
Upper Hill Street 15 D5
Upper Thornton Road......16 E1
Vaynor Road 16 F5
Vicary Crescent 16 G6
Vicary Street......16 G6
Victoria Road 16 E5
Vivian Drive......15 D5
Warrior Way 16 H3
Warwick Road......16 F5

Waterloo Road 15 D5
Wellington Gardens 15 D6
Wellington Road......15 D5
Wellington Square 15 D6
Westaway Drive 15 C6
Westfield Drive 16 G3
Westhill Avenue 16 F4
Willow End 16 G4
Windmill Villas 15 A5
Woodbine Way 15 B4
Woodlands Crescent 16 G4
Woodlands Drive 16 G4
Yorke Close......16 F5
Yorke Street 16 F5

NARBERTH
ARBERTH

Adams Drive 30 F5
Back Lane*, High Street 30 F5
Beechwood Place 30 F4
Belmore Gardens 30 F5
Bentley Villas 30 G5
Bloomfield Gardens 30 F4
Bridge Hill 30 F6
Bridge Villas 30 E6
Brookside Caravan Park......30 F6
Bushes Lane 30 F5
Carding Mill Lane 30 E5
Castle Lane......30 F6
Castle Terrace......30 E5
Castle View 30 F6
Cawdor Court*, James John Cl.
  ......30 F5
Chapelfield Gardens 30 F5
Church Street 30 F6
Coxhill 30 E5
Crescent, The 30 F5
Croft Villas 30 F5
De Rutzen Flats 30 F5
Drang, The*, James John Close
  ......30 F5
Garfield Gardens 30 E6
Green Gardens*, Castle St. 30 F6
Halkon Crescent 30 F5
Hawthorns, The 30 E4
High Street 30 F5
Highfield Park 30 E5
Hill Park......30 E5
Hillside Terrace*, The Hawthorns
  ......30 E5
James John Close 30 F5
Jesse Road 30 F5
John Morgan Close 30 G5
Kiln Park Road 30 H5
Kings Court 30 F5
Landsker Lane 30 F4
Market Square......30 F5
Market Street......30 F5
Mill Lane 30 F6
Mill Pond Road 30 F6
Millfarm Cottages 30 F6
Moorfield 30 E5
Moorfield Road 30 E4
Nestor Square 30 F5
Northfield Court 30 F5
Northfield Road 30 F5
Northmead 30 G5
Old Keg Yard......30 F5
Orchard Court 30 H5
Panteg Uchaf 30 H5
Parc Roberts 30 E4

Park Terrace 30 E5
Picton Place 30 F5
Picton Terrace 30 F5
Queens Street 30 F5
Railway Terrace 30 H5
Redstone Road 30 F4
Rushacre Road......30 E4
Southmead 30 G5
Spring Gardens 30 F5
Springfield Park 30 G4
St. James Street 30 G4
Starlings Park*, St. James Street
  ......30 F5
Station Approach 30 H5
Station Road 30 G5/H5
Sunnybank Home 30 F4
Tabernacle Lane 30 F5
Tabernacle Row 30 F5
Town Houses*, High St. 30 F5
Valley Road......30 E6
Victoria Close 30 F5
Water Street 30 F5
Wells Road Terrace 30 E5
Wesley Villas 30 G5
Westfield Court 30 E5
Williams Court 30 F4

NEWCASTLE
EMLYN

Aber Arad Road 31 C3
Ardwyn Terrace 31 B2
Blaenwern 31 B2
Bridge Street 31 B2
Bryn Deri Close......31 B1
Bryn Farm Road 31 A2
Cardigan Road 31 A2
Carmarthen Road 31 D2
Castle Street 31 B2
Castle Terrace 31 B2
Cawdor Terrace 31 B2
Church Lane 31 B2
Coedmor Lane 31 B1
Coedmor Terrace 31 B1
College Street 31 B2
Cwm Cych Road......31 A3
Cwm Sarah Road 31 A3
Derby Lane 31 B2
Derwen Gardens......31 B1
Ebenezer Street 31 B3
Emlyn Square 31 B2
Emlyn Villas 31 C3
Ffinant Square 31 B3
Garregwen 31 B1
Glaspant Terrace 31 C3
Glazier Row 31 B3
Graig Villas*, Old Graig St. ..31 B3
Heol Brynarian 31 B3
Heol y Ffinant 31 B3
Heol y Gof 31 B3
High Street 31 B3
Llandyfriog Road......31 B2
Lloyds Terrace 31 B1
Maes Llewelyn 31 B2
Maes Marlog 31 C3
Market Place 31 B2
Market Square 31 B2
Mill Street 31 C3
Min y Dre......31 B2
New Road 31 A2
Old Carmarthen Road 31 C3
Old Graig Street 31 B3

Parc Hafen 31 B2
Parc Johnson 31 B3
Parcytrap Road 31 B1
Penlan Road 31 B3
Penlon Terrace 31 B3
Pentre Hedyn 31 B1
Persondy......31 C3
Porth Street 31 B3
Quarry Ffinant 31 B3
Quarry Ffinant 31 B3
Station Road 31 C3
Station Terrace 31 C3
Sycamore Street 31 B2
Tanyard Lane 31 B3
Tivy Terrace 31 B2
Water Street 31 B3
Woodburn Terrace 31 C3

NEWPORT

Banc Cottages 31 C5
Bank Terrace 31 C5
Bentick Terrace......31 C5
Berrymen Terrace......31 B5
Bridge Street......31 C5
Bromeddyg 31 C4
Cambria Terrace......31 C5
Carreg Coetan 31 C5
Castle Street......31 C5
Church Street 31 C5
Coedmore 31 C5
College Square 31 C5
East Street 31 C5
Feidr Bentick......31 C5
Feidr Brenin 31 A5
Feidr Eglwys......31 C6
Feidr Fach......31 C4
Feidr Felin......31 A5
Feidr Ganol 31 A5
Feidr Pen y Bont......31 A5
Ffordd Bedd Morris......31 A6
Ffordd Cilgwyn 31 D6
Fishguard Road 31 A5
Glan y Don 31 B4
Goat Street 31 C5
King Street 31 C6
Kings Terrace 31 C6
Lon Las......31 C4
Long Street 31 C5
Lower St. Marys Street......31 C5
Maes Curig 31 B4
Maes Ingli 31 B5
Maes Morfa......31 C5
Maes y Cnwce 31 B5
Market Street 31 C5
Mill Lane 31 C6
Mount Pleasant Terrace 31 A5
Nantyblodau Bach 31 C6
New Road......31 C5
Newport Bay Caravan Park 31 B5
Parrog Road 31 B4
Penrallt Terrace 31 C6
Spring Hill 31 B5
Spring Hill Terrace 31 B4
Tir Treharn 31 B5
Ty Coch......31 B5
Upper Bridge Street 31 C5
Upper St. Marys Street......31 C4
Upper West Street 31 B5
West Street 31 B5
Woodville Terrace......31 C5

Albion Terrace.....

NEW QUAY
CEI NEWYDD

Albion Terrace......................32 F1
Bellevue 32 G3
Brongwyn Lane 32 G2
Church Road.........................32 F2
Church Street 32 G1
Cromer Crescent 32 G2
Cwm Halen 32 H3
Cwm Ifor 32 G2
Cylch y Llan 32 F1
Field Place 32 G2
Francis Street 32 F3
George Street........................32 G2
Glanmor Terrace 32 G2
Gomer Crescent*, Glanmor Ter.
....32 G2
Hengall Uchaf......................32 H3
Heol y Cwm 32 G2
High Street 32 G1
High Terrace.........................32 G2
Hill Street.............................32 F1
Lewis Terrace 32 F1
Llandysul Road.....................32 F3
Margaret Street 32 G2
Marine Terrace 32 G1
Masons Square......................32 F1
Morfa Gwyn 32 G2
Neuadd Caravan Park 32 F1
Park Street 32 G2
Penrhiw Pistyll Caravan Park
....32 H3
Penrhiw Pistyll Lane.............32 G3
Pentre Garth 32 G2
Penwig Fields 32 F2
Penwig Lane.........................32 G1
Picton Crescent 32 G1
Picton Terrace 32 G2
Pilot Lane 32 G2
Porth yr Eglwys....................32 F2
Prospect Place*, Wellington Pl.
....32 G1
Queen Street 32 G2
Rectory Square 32 F2
Rock Street............................32 G1
School Lane 32 G2
Schooner Caravan Park........32 H3
South John Street 32 G1
Spring Gardens*, Church Street
....32 G1
Stone Court...........................32 F1
Tower Hill 32 F1
Towyn Road 32 F2
Uplands Square 32 F2
Water Street 32 F1
Wellington Place...................32 G1
White Street 32 G1

NEYLAND

Barnlake Point 32 H5
Belle Vue Street 32 F5
Blenheim Drive 32 G4
Bluebell Close 32 F4
Brunel Avenue......................32 F6
Brunel Quay 32 G6
Cambrian Road 32 G6
Charles Street 32 F5
Church Lake Terrace 32 F5
Church Road.........................32 E6
Church Way 32 F6
Cleddau Avenue 32 F5

College Park 32 G6
Coram Drive 32 G4
Crossways 32 E4
Dolphin Court 32 G6
Elm Grove 32 F4
Fern Rise 32 F5
Field Cottages 32 G6
Fleming Way 32 F4
Frederick Street 32 G5
Gaddarn Reach 32 G5
George Street 32 F5
Glen Owen Hill 32 E4
Glen Villas............................32 E4
Gordon Parry Close 32 F5
Gordon Parry Road...............32 F5
Gothic Road 32 F5
Great Eastern Terrace 32 G6
Green Lane............................32 G6
Harbour Close 32 F5
High Street 32 G5
Hill Terrace 32 G6
Honeyborough Farm Cottages
....32 F5
Honeyborough Green 32 F4
Honeyborough Grove 32 F4
Honeyborough Road..............32 F4
Jackson Drive 32 G4
James Street 32 F5
John Street 32 G5
Kensington Road 32 F5
Lawrenny Street 32 G6
Leonardston Road 32 E5
Leonardston View 32 F5
Mayfield Road.......................32 G5
Military Road 32 E5
Mill Drive 32 G4
Mount Pleasant.....................32 H5
Neyland Heights 32 F5
Neyland Hill 32 G6
Neyland Vale 32 F5
Osborn Close 32 G5
Osborn Park 32 G5
Phillips Walk 32 E5
Picton Road 32 G6
Poppy Drive 32 G4
Primrose Close 32 G4
Promenade Close 32 F6
Promenade Drive 32 F6
Promenade, The 32 F6
Queen Elizabeth Avenue 32 F6
Railway Terrace 32 G6
Riga Avenue 32 F6
Riverside Avenue 32 F6
Rock Cottages 32 F5
Rumsey Drive 32 G4
Scurlock Drive 32 G4
Sidney Webb Close 32 F6
Sports Way 32 G5
Springfield Avenue 32 F5
Springfield Close 32 G5
St. Annes Place.....................32 F6
St. Clements Road 32 G6
Station Road 32 G6
Trafalgar Terrace 32 F6
Trinity Place 32 F6
Vale Road 32 F5
Victoria Court 32 F5
West Lane 32 F4
Westfield Close 32 F4
Windsor Gardens 32 G5
Wood Lane 32 F4
Woodland Park 32 F5

PEMBROKE

Adams Road 23 B1
Angle Road 23 C1
Ashdale Lane 23 B4
Ashleigh Gardens 23 C5
Back Lane 23 B2
Back Terrace 23 B2
Beaufort Road.......................23 A4
Belmont Terrace 23 C5
Bengal Villas 23 B5
Bishops Lane 23 C6
Bishops Park.........................23 C6
Bridgend Terrace 23 B3
Brockfield Lane 23 D5
Bush Hill 23 A3
Buttermilk Close 23 A3
Buttermilk Lane 23 A4
Callans Drive 23 B6
Castle Terrace 23 B3
Castle View 23 A3
Charles Road 23 B5
Church Terrace 23 B2
Clare Walk 23 A4
Coldwell Terrace 23 A3
Colley Court 23 B1
Common Road 23 B3/B4
Cooks Close 23 B6
Court Terrace 23 B3
Crick Marren Close...............23 C6
Croeso Road..........................23 C5
Croft Court 23 B3
Cromwell Cottages*,
   Westgate Hill 23 B3
Cromwell Court 23 C5
Devon Drive 23 A3
East Back 23 B4
Elm Grove 23 A3
First Lane 23 B5
Fourth Lane 23 C6
Freemans Walk 23 C5
Froynes Terrace 23 C4
Giddas Lane 23 C6
Golden Brake 23 B5
Golden Cottages 23 B4
Golden Hill Road..................23 B3
Golden Lane 23 B4
Gooses Lane 23 C4
Green Meadow Avenue 23 A3
Green, The 23 B3
Grove Bridge.........................23 C4
Grove Bridge Cottages 23 C4
Grove Drive 23 D4
Grove Green 23 C4
Grove Hill 23 C4
Grove Way 23 D4
Grove, The 23 C4
Gwilliam Court......................23 B1
Hamilton Terrace 23 B4
Harcourt Terrace 23 B4
Haven Court 23 B1
Herons Reach 23 B4
Holyland Road 23 B5
Howells Close 23 B1
Hywel Way 23 C3
India Row 23 B1
Jogram Avenue 23 B1
Kingsbridge Cottages 23 B5
Kingsbridge Drive 23 B5
Laugharne Close 23 A4
Lewis Terrace 23 B4
Llewellyn Drive 23 C3

Lloyd George Lane................23 C3
Long Mains 23 B1
Lords Meadow View 23 B5
Lower Lamphey Road 23 C4
Lower Row 23 B4
Lowless Close........................23 D4
Main Street 23 B3
Mansel Street 23 B3
Margarets Way 23 C6
Marshall Road.......................23 C6
Merchants Park 23 C2
Merlins Cross 23 C5
Mid Row 23 A4
Mill Brook 23 C1
Mill Pond Walk 23 B3
Monkton Street 23 B3
Montgomery Close 23 B1
New Way...............................23 B4
Nicholls Road 23 C6
Norgans Hill 23 D2
Norgans Terrace 23 C2
North Gate Street 23 B3
Old Conduit, The 23 C2
Orange Way 23 C4
Orchard Buildings 23 C5
Orchard Gardens 23 B5
Owen Street 23 B3
Parade, The 23 B3
Paradise Row 23 B3
Paynter Street 23 C3
Police Houses 23 B3
Powell Close 23 A4
Poyners Avenue 23 C3
Ramsden Court......................23 B1
Riverside Home 23 B4
Rock Terrace 23 B4
Rocky Park 23 B3
Ropewalk Terrace 23 C5
Rowlands Way 23 C4
School Terrace 23 B3
Shoulder of Lamb 23 B4
South Meadows 23 C3
South Mews 23 C3
South Road 23 C3
South Terrace 23 C2
Southdown Close 23 C3
Southlands 23 C3
St. Anns Crescent 23 B3
St. Daniels Drive 23 C3
St. Daniels Hill 23 D3
St. Davids Road 23 C6
St. Martins Road 23 B1
St. Michaels Road 23 C6
St. Nicholas Crescent 23 A3
St. Petrox Close 23 B4
St. Twynnells Close 23 C4
Station Road 23 C4
Strongbow Walk 23 A3
Tenby Court 23 B1
Third Lane 23 C6
Thomas Street 23 C3
Treleet Cottages 23 C5
Tudor Close 23 C4
Twopenny Hay Close 23 B5
Upper Lamphey Road 23 C5
Upper Row 23 A4
Valence Walk 23 A3
Vetch Close 23 C3
Vicarage Field 23 C5
Victoria Terrace.....................23 A4
Wades Close..........................23 B5
Watery Lane 23 C5

Webbs Drive 23 C3
Well Hill...............................23 C4
West Street 23 C3
Westgate Court*, Westgate Hill
....23 B3
Westgate Hill.......................23 B3
Wheelers Way 23 C4
Whitehall Avenue 23 A3
Whitehall Drive 23 A3
Williamson Street 23 C3
Windsor Road 23 B4
Wiston Street 23 A4
Wogan Road........................23 B3
Woodbine Close 23 B4
Woodbine Terrace 23 B3
Woodside Avenue 23 A3
Wrench Close......................23 C4

PEMBROKE DOCK

Admiralty Way 17 D3
Afton Court 17 D3
Albany Street 18 E5
Albion Square 18 E3
Amphion Court 18 G4
Apley Terrace 18 F3
Argyle Street 18 E3
Arthur Morris Drive 18 E5
Arthur Street 18 E3
Beach Road 17 B3
Beaufort Road (Pemb.) 18 H6
Belle Vue Terrace...............17 D4
Bentlass Terrace 17 D5
Benton Court 17 D3
Bethel Road 18 G4
Bierspool 18 F3
Birdcage Walk.....................18 F4
Brewery Street 18 E3
Britannia Drive 18 E5
Britannia Road 18 E4
Bufferland Terrace 18 E4
Bush Hill (Pembroke).........18 H5
Bush Street 18 E3/G4
Buttermilk Close (Pemb.) 18 H5
Buttermilk Lane (Pemb.).....18 H5
Cannons Lane 17 D5
Canterbury Road 18 F2
Canton Court 17 D3
Carr Terrace 17 D5
Castle Street........................17 D6
Castle View (Pembroke) 18 H6
Catalonia Avenue 17 D3
Cenarth Close 18 G2
Chapel Road........................17 C3
Charles Thomas Avenue 18 F3
Charlton Place 18 E4
Cheriton Road 17 D5
Church Street 18 E4
Clare Walk (Pembroke) 18 H6
Clarence Street....................18 E3
Co Op Lane 17 D4
Coldwell Terrace (Pemb.) ..18 H6
Commercial Row 17 D3
Connaught Place 18 F2
Corporation Terrace 18 E4
Criterion Way 18 E2
Croft Terrace.......................18 E4
Croft, The (Pembroke) 18 H6
Cromwell Street...................18 F3
Cross Park 17 D4
Cumby Terrace....................17 D3

Dayton Court.......................17 D3
Devon Drive (Pembroke) 18 H5
Devonshire Road 18 F2
Dimond Street......................18 E3
Donovan Reed Gardens 18 F3
Dorset Row 18 F2
Eastern Avenue 18 G3
Eaton Court.........................17 D3
Edgar Morgan Way.............17 C3
Elm Terrace (Pembroke) 18 H6
Essex Road 18 F2
Fairway 17 D4
Fenton Court 17 D3
Ferry Lane 18 G4
Ferry Road 17 D6
Ferry Terrace 18 G3
Finch Close 18 E5
Fleet Street 17 D6
Fort Road 17 C3
Front Street 18 E4
Furzy Bank 18 E5
Gables, The*, Queen St. 18 E3
Gays Lane 17 D5
Gilgal Terrace 17 D5
Glenview Avenue 18 F2
Gloucester Way 18 F2
Golden Hill Road (Pemb.) ..18 H6
Gordon Street 18 E3
Gorton Court 17 D3
Gothic Cottages 17 D5
Gravel Lane 18 E3
Green Meadow Avenue (Pemb.)
....18 H6
Greenhill Road 18 H6
Grove Street.............17 D6/18 E6
Gwyther Street 18 E4
Hamilton Close 17 D5
Hamilton Court 18 G4
Hampshire Drive 18 F2
Harbour Way.......................18 E3
Haven Drive 17 A4
Hawkstone Road................18 F3
High Street (Neyland) 18 E1
High Street (Pemb. Dock)...18 E4
High Street Close 18 E4
Hill Farm Caravan Park 18 E5
Hill Street............................18 E5
Hill Terrace (Neyland) 18 E1
Imble Close 18 F4
Imble Street.........................18 E5
Kavanagh Court 18 G4
Kent Row 18 F2
King Street 18 E3
King William Street 18 F3
Kings Gardens 17 D5
Kitchener Close 17 D4
Lavinia Drive 18 G3
Laws Street 18 E3/E4
Lewis Street 18 E3
Llanion Cottages 18 G3
London Road.................18 F3/G3
London Road Mall 18 G3
Long Mains 18 F6
Lower Row (Pembroke) 18 H6
Market Place 17 D3
Market Street 17 D4
Melville Street 18 E5
Melville Terrace 17 D3
Meyrick Owen Way.............17 D3
Meyrick Street 18 E4
Mid Row (Pembroke) 18 H6
Military Road 17 B4

Milton Terrace 18 E4
Munro Court 18 G4
Nelson Street 17 D5
Neyland Hill (Neyland) 18 E1
Neyland Terrace (Neyland) .18 E1
North Street.........................18 E4
Oak Road 17 D5
Ocean Way 17 A4
Orielton Terrace 17 C3
Owen Street 17 D4
Paradise Row (Pembroke) ..18 H6
Park Lane 18 E3
Park Street 18 E4
Park View Crescent 18 F4
Paterchurch 17 C3
Paterchurch Road...............18 H3
Pembroke Ferry 18 G1
Pembroke Haven*, Essex Road
....18 F2
Pembroke Road 18 E4
Pembroke Street.................17 D4
Pembroke Villas 18 E4
Phillips Lane 17 D5
Picton Place 18 E4
Picton Road (Neyland) 18 E1
Pier Road 18 E2
Presely View 17 C3
Princess Street 17 D3
Prospect Place 18 E4
Queen Square Mews 18 E3
Queen Street 18 E3
Richmond Road 18 E2
Rocky Park (Pembroke) 18 H6
School Gardens 17 D5
Shropshire Road 18 G2
Southampton Row 17 D3
Springfield Road 18 F5
St. Andrews Road 18 F3
St. Anns Crescent (Pembroke)
....18 H6
St. Clements Road (Neyland)
....18 E1
St. Johns Road 18 F4
St. Marys Road 18 F3
St. Nicholas Close (Pemb.) .18 H6
St. Patricks Hill 17 C3
St. Patricks Road 18 F4
St. Peters Road 18 F4
St. Teilos Road 18 F4
Station Road (Neyland) 18 E1
Stockwell Road 18 E2
Stranraer Avenue 17 C5
Stranraer Lane 17 C5
Stranraer Road 17 C5
Strongbow Walk (Pemb.) ...18 H6
Sunderland Avenue 17 D3
Sussex Row 18 F2
Sycamore Street 18 E5
Terrace, The 17 D3
Tregennis Hill Flats.............17 D4
Tremeyrick Street 18 F2
Treowen Road 17 D5
Trinity Road 18 F3
Upper Row (Pembroke) 18 H6
Valence Walk (Pembroke) ..18 H6
Victoria Road 17 D3
Warrior Way 18 G2
Water Street 18 F3
Waterloo Road 18 F1/G2
Wavell Crescent 18 G4
Wellington Street.................18 E3
Wesley Court 18 G4

Western Way 18 E3
Whitehall Avenue (Pembroke)
....18 H6
Whitehall Drive (Pembroke) .18 H6
Whites Farm Way 17 C3
Windsor Road (Pembroke)..18 H6
Wogan Street (Pembroke) ..18 H6
Woodbine Terrace (Pembroke)
....18 H6
Woodside Avenue (Pembroke)
....18 H6

PEN-Y-GROES, CAPEL HENDRE & SARON

Banc y Ddraenen 25 A5
Black Lion Road 25 A4
Blaen Emlyn 25 A1
Blaenau Road 25 C1
Bridge Street 25 A1
Bryn Road 25 A2
Brynawelon 25 D3
Bryncwar Road 25 A2
Bryndedwynddfa 25 A2
Brynderi..............................25 C1
Brynglas 25 B3
Brynteg 25 B6
Caer Bryn Road 25 A2
Caer Bryn Terrace 25 B1
Cefncrug 25 C4
Clos y Cwm.........................25 A4
Clos yr Hendre 25 B5
Coopers Road 25 B6
Cwm Saeson 25 D6
Delfryn 25 B6
Dyffryn Road 25 D4
Fferws Road 25 D5
Garnfoel 25 A3
Gate Road...........................25 A1
Gilfach y Gog 25 A3
Glan Rhyd 25 B5
Gorsddu Road 25 A2
Hendre Road.......................25 B6
Heol Fach 25 C1
Heol Lotwen 25 A6
Llwyn Celyn........................25 B5
Llys Lotwen 25 B6
Maesglas 25 B3
Nant Arw 25 A4
Nant y Ci Road 25 D4
Nant y Dderwen 25 D4
Norton Road 25 A1
Parc Hendre 25 B6
Park Avenue 25 A5
Penygroes Road 25 B1
Plas Gwyn Road 25 A1
Pontblodau Road 25 D2
Rhos Terrace 25 D6
Saron Road 25 B5/D3
Spien Road 25 A3
St. Davids Way 25 A3
Tanyfan 25 B5
Tre Elfred 25 B2
Waterloo Road 25 A2
Waterloo Terrace 25 A5

PONTYBEREM

Ashgrove 24 G5
Bragdu 24 F6
Brandyway 24 F4
Bryn Tirion 24 F5

Caersalem Row.....

Caersalem Row	24 F4
Capel Seion Road	24 E6
Coalbrook Road	24 G5
Dreonen	24 G5
Ffordd Aneurin	24 F3
Furnace Terrace	24 F5
Greenfield Terrace	24 E5
Grugos Avenue	24 F5
Gwendraeth Row	24 G5
Haulfryn	24 E2
Heol Aneddfa	24 F5
Heol Capel Ifan	24 G4/H3
Heol Llethryd	24 F4
Heol y Banc	24 E2
Heol y Bryn	24 E5
Heol y Felin	24 F3
Heol y Parc	24 G4
Heol y Pentre	24 G4
Hewlett Road	24 G4
Llanhir	24 E4
Llannon Road	24 G5
Llwynyeos	24 F3
Maesyderi	24 F6
Maesyfelin	24 F4
Min y Graig	24 E5
Mynachlog Road	24 F4
Mynachlog Terrace	24 F4
Nant y Glo	24 G5
New Road	24 F5
Parc y Mynach	24 F4
Penybryn	24 E1
Railway Terrace	24 G3
Station Road	24 F6
Sylen Road	24 H5
Tyr Heol	24 E3
Water Street	24 F4

SAUNDERSFOOT

Bath Cottages	34 G3
Bedoes Court	34 H2
Belle Vue	34 G1
Bench Court	34 H1
Bethany Flats	34 H2
Bevelin Hall	34 G3
Bevelyn Lane	34 H3
Bonvilles Close	34 F1
Brewery Cottages	34 H2
Brewery Flats	34 H2
Brewery Terrace	34 H2
Broadfield Hill	34 G3
Brookdale	34 G3
Brookland Close	34 H2
Brookland Place	34 H2
Cambrian Terrace	34 H2
Captains Walk	34 H2
Cartref	34 G1
Castle View	34 G1
Church Terrace	34 H1
Coedrath Park	34 G1
Cwm Gwennol	34 H3
Devonshire Drive	34 E3
Dros y Mor	34 G2
Fan Road, The	34 F1
Ferndale	34 G3
Frances Cottages	34 G2
Frances Lane	34 H1
Frances Road	34 H1
Garden Cottage Flats	34 G1
Glen, The	34 H2
Glenvale	34 H3
Gorse Hill	34 G3
Guys Villas	34 G1
Harbour Court	34 H2
Harbour Heights	34 H1
Hean Close	34 G1
High Street	34 H1
Hill Cottages	34 H2
Hillside Cottages	34 G3
Holmlea Court	34 H1
Hopshill Lane	34 E3
Incline Way	34 F1/G2
Incline, The	34 F1
Lantern Court	34 H2
Lawnswood	34 G2
Malin Court	34 H2
Milford Street	34 H2
Milford Terrace	34 H2
Monkstone Court	34 H2
Monkstone View	34 H1
Narbeth Road	34 E3
Nash Place	34 G1
North Close	34 F1
Nyth Gwennol	34 G3
Oakhill Drive	34 G3
Pennant Avenue	34 G1
Plantation Cottages	34 G3
Pyatts Nest	34 G1
Ragged Staff	34 G2
Rainbow Vale	34 H2
Rhodewood Terrace	34 H3
Ridgeway Close	34 G1
Ridgeway Meadows	34 G1
Ridgeway, The	34 F1
Rosemount	34 G1
Rosewood Cottages	34 G1
Rushylake	34 G3
Sandy Hill Park	34 G3
Sandy Hill Road	34 F3
Scandanavia Heights	34 G3
Southfield Villas	34 H2
St. Brides Gardens	34 H2
St. Brides Hill	34 H3
St. Brides Lane	34 H2
Stammers Court	34 G3
Stammers Lane	34 G3
Stammers Road	34 G2
Strand, The	34 H1
Strandway Court	34 H1
Strathyre Court	34 G2
Swallow Dale	34 G3
Valley Road	34 E1
Vanderhoof Way	34 G1
Westfield Court	34 G1
Westfield Road	34 G1
White Park Bungalows	34 F1
Whitlow	34 G1
Windsor Terrace	34 G1
Wogan Lane	34 H1
Wogan Terrace	34 H1

ST. CLEARS
SANCLER

Backe Road	33 A3
Bethlehem Road	33 A1/A2
Bridge Street	33 C3
Britannia Terrace	33 B2
Bryncaredig	33 C2
Carmarthen Road	33 D2
Castle Cottages	33 C2
Clare Hill	33 A1
Clos Nathaniel	33 A1
Clos y Drindod	33 D1
Corvus Terrace	33 D2
Craig Villas	33 C3
Croft Cottages	33 C3
Dol y Felin	33 D2
Ffynnongain Lane	33 A1
Foxhole Terrace	33 C3
Gardde Fields	33 C2
Gelli	33 A3
Gerddi Mair	33 B3
Gors Fach	33 A1
Green Park Terrace	33 C3
Heol Gerig	33 A3
Heol Goi	33 C3
Heol Llaindelyn	33 A2
High Street	33 C2
Island Terrace	33 A2
Kieffe Terrace	33 C3
Kingswood Terrace	33 D1
Lon Fair	33 C3
Lon Hafren	33 D1
Lon Las	33 A1
Lon Llysalaw	33 A1
Lon y Prior	33 C1
Lower Ostrey	33 C1
Osborne Terrace	33 D3
Ostrey Bank	33 B2
Pandy Grove	33 C2
Pen y Fford	33 C2
Pentre Road	33 C2
Pleasant View	33 C2
Rhyd y Gors	33 D1
Riverside Terrace	33 D3
Spring Gardens	33 A1
Springfield	33 C1
Station Road	33 D1
Tenby Road	33 B2
Tir Owen	33 C1
Wembley Place	33 D1
Wembly Gardens	33 D2
Ysgubor Fawr	33 A1

ST. DAVID'S
TY DDEWI

Bryn Road	33 B5
Brynteg	33 B6
Catherine Street	33 B5
Cross Square	33 B5
Feidr Chwech Erw	33 A4/A5
Feidr Pant y Bryn	33 C6
Feidr Treginnis	33 A5
Ffordd Caerfai	33 C6
Ffordd Melin Isaf	33 A5
Ffordd Owen	33 B5
Ffordd Porth Clais	33 A6
Ffos y Mynach	33 D5
Ffynnon Wen	33 B6
Glasfryn Lane	33 C5
Glasfryn Road	33 C5
Goat Street	33 B5
Gospel Lane	33 B5
Heol Dewi	33 C5
High Street	33 C5
Llys Dewi	33 C5
Maes Dewi	33 C5
Maes Dyfed	33 C5
Maes Elfed	33 C5
Maes y Dre	33 C6
Maes y Hedydd	33 C5
Maes y Mynach	33 D5
Meidr Dwyll	33 B4
Millard Park	33 C5
Mitre Lane	33 B5
Mount Gardens	33 C4
New Street	33 C5
Noddfa Dewi	33 C5
Nun Street	33 B5
Pebbles, The	33 B5
Pen Rhiw	33 B4
Pen y Garn	33 B5
Peters Lane	33 C5
Pigfoot Lane	33 B5
Pit Street	33 B5
Quickwell Hill	33 B4
Ramsey Gardens	33 A6
St. Nons Close	33 B5
Steps Lane	33 B5
Tower Hill	33 B5
Town Hall Lane	33 C5
Waun Isaf	33 A6
Yr Hafan	33 B6

ST. FLORENCE

Eastern Lane	37 A3
Elm View	37 B2
Flemish Close	37 B2
Flemish Court	37 B2
Green Hayes Avenue	37 A3
Grove Court	37 A2
High Street	37 A2
Longstone	37 A2
Morgans Terrace	37 A3
Parklands	37 A1
Parsons Green	37 A2
Ridgeway, The	37 A2
St. Florence Cottages	37 B1

TENBY
DINBYCH-Y-PYSGOD

Acorn Heights	26 G3
Alma Flats (Penally)	26 H6
Alma Gardens (Penally)	26 G6
Augustus Place	26 G3
Bank Lane	26 G3
Barrington House*, South Cliffe Street	26 G4
Battery Road	26 G2
Belle Vue Cottages*, Crackwell Street	26 G3
Belmont Court	26 F3
Blind Lane	26 F1/F2
Bridge Street	26 H3
Broadwell Hayes	26 F2
Brynhir	26 F1
Burrows, The	26 F4
Cambrian Cottages	26 F2
Castle Square	26 H3
Church Park	26 G4
Church Street	26 G4
Churchill Close	26 E3
Clareston Court*, Station Road	26 G3
Clareston Road	26 G3
Clement Terrace	26 G3
Clickett Lane	26 E3
Clicketts Court	26 E3
Coastguard Houses*, Broadwell Hayes	26 F2
Cob Lane	26 H4
Coupland Villas	26 F3
Crackwell Close	26 G6
Crackwell Lane*, Crackwell St.	26 G3
Crackwell Street	26 G3

Cresswell Court*, Cresswell St.
...................................26 H4
Cresswell Street 26 H4
Croft Court 26 G2
Croft Terrace 26 G2
Croft, The 26 G3
Crows Nest 26 H6
Culver Park 26 G4
Deer Park 26 G3
Deer Park Villas 26 G3
Edward Street 26 G4
Esplanade 26 G4
Fourwinds Lane 26 H5
Frogmore Terrace*,
    Lower Frog Street 26 G4
Gas Lane 26 G2
Giltar Terrace (Penally) 26 H6
Giltar Way 26 G6
Glan y Mor Court*,
    Strawberry Lane 26 H6
Glas Nevin Gardens 26 F2
Glebe, The 26 G2
Glen View Crescent 26 F2
Green Crescent 26 G3
Green, The 26 F3
Greenhill Avenue 26 G3
Greenhill Road 26 G3
Hamilton Court*, Upper Park Rd.
...................................26 G3
Hanover Court 26 G4
Harding Street 26 G3
Harding Villas*, Harding St. ..26 G3
Harries Street 26 G4
Haytor Gardens.....................26 F2
Heywood Court 26 F2
Heywood Lane 26 E3
High Street 26 G3
Hill Farm Road (Penally) 26 G6
Hill Park 26 F2
Holloway Court (Penally) 26 H5
Holloway Hill (Penally) 26 G5
Hoyles Close (Penally) 26 H5
Ivy Cottages 26 H4
Jones Terrace........................26 G3
Jubilee Cottages 26 F2
Kenystyle (Penally)...............26 H5
Knowling Mead 26 E3
Lady Park 26 F1/F2
Lamack Vale 26 E2
Lansdowne Cottages*,
    St. Julians Street............26 H4
Laxton Flats 26 H3
Leach Way 26 F2
Lexden Terrace 26 H4
Longfield 26 H5
Lower Frog Street..................26 G4
Lower Park Road 26 F3
Marsh Road 26 E3
Marsh Road Cottages...........26 F3
Maudlins 26 F2
Maudlins Villas 26 F2
Mayfield Drive 26 G2
Merlins Court 26 G3
Merlins Gardens 26 G2
Mews,The*, South Parade ..26 G3
Middle Walls Lane (Penally)
...................................26 H5
Montrose 26 H6
Narberth Road.......................26 F1
Newell Hill 26 F3
Norton 26 G2
Norton Cottages 26 G3

Oakridge Acres 26 E3
Old Narbeth Road 26 F1
Paddock, The (Penally) 26 H5
Paddock, The (Tenby) 26 F2
Paragon 26 H4
Paragon Court 26 H4
Park Place 26 G4
Park Road..............................26 G3
Park Terrace 26 G4
Penally Heights 26 G6
Penally Road 26 G3
Penniless Cove Hill...............26 H3
Picton Road 26 G4
Picton Terrace 26 G4
Pier Hill 26 H3
Police Flats*, Augustus Pl. ..26 G3
Promenade 26 G3
Quarry Cottages 26 G4
Quay Hill 26 H3
Queens Parade 26 G4
Queensfield 26 E3
Rectory Court 26 G3
Regency Court 26 G3
Retreat Road 26 H5
Ridgeway, The 26 G5
Rock Houses 26 G4
Rock Terrace 26 H4
Rocky Park 26 G3
Rosemount Court*,
    Rosemount Gardens 26 F3
Rosemount Garden Villas 26 F3
Rosemount Gardens.............26 F3
Royal Victoria Court 26 G3
Salterns, The.........................26 F4
School Lane 26 E5/H5
Scotsborough View 26 E3
Sea Vista 26 H5
Seagarth*, St. Julians St. 26 H4
Seascape 26 F2
Sergeants Lane*, St. Julians St.
...................................26 H4
Serpentine Gardens 26 E3
Serpentine Road 26 F3
Silven Flats 26 G2
Slippery Back 26 F3
Somerset Place*, Park Road
...................................26 G3
South Cliffe Gardens 26 G4
South Cliffe Street 26 G4
South Parade 26 G3
Southlands 26 F2
Sperricomb Lane 26 F1
St. Catherines Terrace 26 H3
St. Davids Close 26 E3
St. Florence Parade 26 G4
St. Georges Street 26 G3
St. Johns Croft*, St. Johns Hill
...................................26 G3
St. Johns Hill 26 G3
St. Julians Street...................26 H3
St. Julians Terrace 26 H3
St. Marys Court*, St. Marys St.
...................................26 G4
St. Marys Street 26 G4
St. Nicholas Crescent (Penally)
...................................26 H5
St. Nicholas Lane*, High St. 26 G3
Station Road 26 G4
Strawberry Gardens (Penally)
...................................26 H6
Strawberry Lane (Penally) ..26 H6
Sutton Street..........................26 G4

Tarporley Cottages*, Augustus Pl.
...................................26 G3
Tenby Close*, Tudor Sq. ...26 H4
Tor Lane*, Cob Lane 26 H4
Town Hall Arcade*,
    Upper Frog Street........26 H3
Trafalgar Road 26 G4
Tudor Square 26 H3
Tudor Way 26 E3
Tysellis Court*, Park Pl. 26 G6
Upper Frog Street..................26 G3
Upper Hill Park 26 F2
Upper Park Road 26 E3
Victoria Cottages 26 E3
Victoria Street 26 G4
Wallsfield Lane 26 G3
Warren Street 26 G3
Waterwynch Lane..................26 G1
Weston Terrace 26 G3
White Lion Street 26 G3
Wimbledon 26 G4
Zion Gardens 26 G3

TREGARON

Bryn Heulog 37 D1
Chapel Street 37 C2
Chapel Street Flats*, Chapel St.
...................................37 C2
Cross Street 37 C2
Currier Street 37 C2
Dewi Road 37 C3
Gardens View 37 D2
Glangro 37 C2
Glanllyn 37 D2
Heol Pontrhydpendigaid 37 D2
Heol y Mynydd 37 D2
High Street 37 D2
Lampeter Road 37 C3
Llar Villas*, Rose Terrace....37 C2
Llys Einon 37 D1
Lon Caron 37 D1
Lon y Ficerdy 37 D1
Lon yr Ystrad Maesamlwg ..37 C2
Maesamlwg............................37 D2
Maesyawel 37 D2
Parc Modur 37 D2
Penrodyn 37 D2
Pleasant Place 37 D2
Pwllswyddog 37 D1
Rhyd y Fawnog......................37 D1
Rose Terrace 37 C2
Square, The 37 D2
Station Road 37 C2
Well Street 37 C2
Ystrad yr Orsaf 37 D1

TUMBLE
Y TYMBL

Banc y Gors 34 G6
Bethania Road 34 G5
Bethesda Road 34 E5
Bryntawel 34 G5
Craig y Lletty.........................34 G6
Darren Las 34 G6
Derwen Road 34 E4
Gors Road 34 G6
Gwendraeth Road..................34 E4
Heol Bryngwili 34 H4
Heol Hirwaun Olau 34 F4
Heol y Bryn 34 G5
Heol y Neuadd 34 F4

High Street 34 F5
Kew Gardens 34 H5
Llannon Road 34 G6
Llechyfedach.........................34 H4
Lletty Road 34 G6
Llys Bethesda 34 F4
Maesgwern 34 E4
Penparc 34 F5
Railway Place 34 F5
Railway Terrace 34 F5
Ravelston Court 34 F4
Rhoslan 34 G5
Rhosnewydd 34 E4
Rhosyderi 34 E4
Singleton Road......................34 G5
Station View 34 E4
Tir Becca 34 F5
Troedy Bryn 34 G6
Tyisha Road 34 F5

WHITLAND
HENDY-GWYN

Bryngwenllian 35 C2
Clos Llwyn Ty Gwyn 35 D1
Cross Street 35 B2
Dairy Cottages 35 B2
Gladstone Terrace 35 B3
Glendale Terrace 35 B3
Intermediate Terrace 35 B2
King Edward Street...............35 B2
Llangan Road 35 B2
Llys y Crofft 35 D1
Lon Hywel 35 A1
Market Street 35 B2
Millbrook 35 B2
Millfield 35 B3
North Road 35 B1
Park Street 35 B2
Rose Cottages 35 C1
Spring Gardens.............35 C2/D2
St. Davids Avenue 35 B2
St. Georges Avenue 35 B3
St. Johns Street 35 B3
St. Mary Street 35 B2
Station Road 35 B2
Trevaughan Gardens 35 B3
Trevaughan Lodge Road 35 B3
Velfrey Road 35 A3
West Street 35 A2
Westover Caravan Park 35 A2
Willow Park 35 B2

HOSPITALS

Aberaeron Cottage Hosp.....27 C1
Amman Valley Hospital.......22 F2
Bronglais Hospital 7 C2
Cardigan Hospital 19 C5
Llandovery Hospital 29 B4
New Tenby Cottage Hosp...26 G2
South Pembrokeshire Hosp.17 C3
St. David's Hospital............11 A3
Tregaron Hospital 37 C3
West Wales General Hosp. 12 H1
Withybush General Hosp.....13 B5

POLICE STATIONS

Aberaeron Police Station 27 C1
Aberystwyth Police Station 7 B3
Ammanford Police Station ..10 E3
Cardigan Police Station 19 C4
Carmarthen Police Station ..11 D4

Cross Hands Police Station.....

Cross Hands Police Station **20** E4
Dyfed Powys Police HQ **12** H4
Fishguard Police Station.......**21** C4
Haverfordwest Police Station
....**14** E3
Lampeter Police Station **28** F5
Llandeilo Police Station **29** B2
Llandovery Police Station **29** B5
Llandysul Police Station **37** D5
Milford Haven Police Station
....**16** F5
Narberth Police Station **30** G5
Newcastle Emlyn Police Station
....**31** B2
Pembroke Dock Police Station
....**18** F3
Saundersfoot Police Station
....**34** H1
St. Clears Police Station.......**33** D1
St. David's Police Station **33** C5
Tenby Police Station **26** G3
Tregaron Police Station **37** C3
Whitland Police Station........**35** B2

TOURIST INFORMATION CENTRES

Aberaeron TIC
Tel. 01545 570602 ......**27** B1
Aberystwyth TIC
Tel. 01970 612125 ....**7** B2
Cardigan TIC
Tel. 01239 613230 ......**19** B4
Carmarthen TIC
Tel. 01267 231557 ......**11** D3
Fishguard Harbour TIC
Tel. 01348 872037 ......**21** B2
Fishguard TIC
Tel. 01348 873484 ......**21** C5
Haverfordwest TIC
Tel. 01437 763110 ......**13** D5
Kilgetty TIC
Tel. 01834 814161 ......**36** E2
Llandovery TIC
Tel. 01550 720693 ......**29** B6
Milford Haven TIC
Tel. 01646 690866 ......**16** E5
New Quay TIC
Tel. 01545 560865 ......**32** G1
Pembroke Dock TIC
Tel. 01646 622753 ......**17** D2
Pembroke Visitor Centre
Tel. 01646 622388 ......**23** B3
Pembrokeshire Coast
National Park
Tel. 01239 820912 ......**31** C5
Saundersfoot TIC
Tel. 01834 813672 ......**34** H2
St. David's TIC
Tel. 01437 720392 ......**33** C5
Tenby TIC
Tel. 01834 842404 ......**26** G4

SCHOOLS & COLLEGES

Aberaeron Primary School ..**27** B2
Aberporth Primary School ..**35** A5
Albion Square Inf. School ...**18** E3
Amman Valley School **10** E2
Ammanford Infants School ..**10** F2
Ammanford Junior School ..**10** E3
Bancffosfelen Primary School
....**24** E1
Betws Primary School..........**10** E5
Blaenau Primary School.......**25** D1
Brynamman Prim. School......**27** C4
Cardigan Infants School **19** C5
Cardigan Junior School **19** C5
Carmarthenshire College of
Technology & Art
(Ammanford Campus) ..**9** C3
Carmarthenshire College of
Technology & Art
(Jobswell Campus) **11** B3
Carmarthenshire College of
Technology & Art
(Pibwrlwyd Campus)....**11** D6
Cefneithin Primary School ..**20** E1
Coleg Ceredigion (Aberystwyth)
....**8** F3
Coleg Ceredigion (Cardigan)
....**19** B5
Cross Hands Prim. School ..**20** G2
Fenton Community Prim. School
....**14** E3
Ferryside Primary School **35** C4
Ffynnonbedr Prim. School ...**28** F5
Fishguard High School **21** C3
Fishguard Holy Name R.C. Sch.
....**21** C3
Fishguard Infants School **21** C4
Fishguard Junior School.......**21** C4
Glan Cleddau School **14** F2
Golden Grove Community School
....**23** B4/C4
Goodwick Primary School ..**21** A1
Gorslas Primary School **20** F4
Greenhill School **26** F3
Hakin Infants School............**15** C5
Hakin Junior School **15** C5
Haverfordwest Education Centre
....**14** E4
Haverfordwest Primary School
....**14** E3
Haylett Grange School **14** H3
Hubberston Prim. School **15** C5
Johnstown Primary School ..**11** B4
Lampeter Comp. Sch. **28** F6
Laugharne School **36** G3
Llandeilo Primary School **29** C2
Llandovery College **29** B5
Llandybie Primary School....**30** F1
Llandysul Primary School **37** C5
Llangadog Primary School ..**36** F5
Llangunnor Primary School **12** E5
Llansteffan Primary School **36** H5
Llechyfedach Prim. School..**34** G5
Mary Immaculate R.C. Sch. **14** F3
Meads Infants School...........**16** F4
Milford Haven Comp. Sch. ..**16** G3
Milford Haven Jun. School ..**16** F4
Model Church in Wales School
....**11** B3
Monkton Priory Prim. Sch. ..**23** B2
Mount Airey Infants School..**14** F4
Mount School, The **16** G4
Myrddin Primary School **11** D2
Narberth Primary School **30** E5
New Quay Primary School...**32** G2
Neyland Infants School........**32** F5
Neyland Junior School **32** G5
Neyland Technical College **32** G6
Parcyrhyn Primary School **9** D4
Pembroke Dock Community Sch.
....**18** F3
Pembroke Dock Nursery School
....**18** F4
Pembroke School **18** G5/**23** A2
Pembrokeshire College **14** F3
Pen-y-Groes Bible College ..**25** B2
Pen-y-Groes Prim. School ..**25** A2
Penally Primary School..**26** E5/H5
Penglais Secondary School ..**8** E2
Pennar Infants School **17** D4
Pennar Primary School **17** C4
Plascrug Primary School **7** C3
Pontyberem Prim. School ..**24** G4
Portfield Special School **14** E2
Prendergast Inf. School **13** C5
Prendergast Junior School ..**13** D5
Queen Elizabeth High Sch. **11** C5
Redhill Preparatory School ..**14** F2
Rhydygors School...............**11** B6
Richmond Park Prim. Sch. ..**12** E2
Saron Primary School..........**25** C4
Saundersfoot Prim. School..**34** H1
Sir Thomas Picton Comp. School
....**13** D5
St. Dogmaels Prim. School **19** C1
St. Florence School **37** A2
St. Francis Primary School ..**16** F4
St. Mark's School **14** G4
St. Mary's R.C. Primary School
(Carmarthen)...............**11** C3
St. Mary's R.C. Primary School
(Pembroke Dock) **18** E4
St. Padarn's Primary School **7** C3
St. Teilo's Primary School ..**26** G3
Stepaside Primary School ..**36** F2
Tasker Milward School **14** E3
Tenby Infants School **26** E3
Tenby Junior School............**26** E2
Tregaron Comp. School **37** C2
Tregaron Primary School **37** D1
Trinity College **11** B3
Tumble Primary School........**34** F4
Tycroes Prim. School..**9** A6/**10** G6
University of Wales, Aberystwyth
(Llanbadarn Campus).....**8** F4
University of Wales, Aberystwyth
(Old College) **7** A2
University of Wales, Aberystwyth
(Penglais Campus) **7** D2
University of Wales, Aberystwyth
(School of Art) **7** C3
University of Wales, Lampeter
....**28** G5
Welsh Institute of Rural Studies
....**8** E4
Ysgol Bro Dewi **33** B5
Ysgol Bro Ingli....................**31** C4
Ysgol Ceredigion **27** C2
Ysgol Comins Coch **8** G1
Ysgol Dewi Sant **33** D5
Ysgol Dyffryn Taf **35** A1
Ysgol Griffith Jones **33** D1
Ysgol Gyfun Aberaeron **27** C2
Ysgol Gyfun Bro Myrddin ..**12** E2
Ysgol Gyfun Dyffryn Teifi ...**37** B5
Ysgol Gyfun Emlyn **31** B3
Ysgol Gyfun Gymunedol
Penweddig **7** D4
Ysgol Gyfun Maes yr Yrfa...**20** F2
Ysgol Gyfun Pantycelyn **29** B5
Ysgol Gymraeg Aberystwyth **7** C3
Ysgol Gymraeg Rhydaman **10** E3
Ysgol Gymunedol Cwmpadarn
....**8** E4
Ysgol Hendy-gwyn **35** B2
Ysgol Llwyn yr Eos **7** D6
Ysgol Rhys Prichard **29** C5
Ysgol Teilo Sant **29** C1
Ysgol Uwchradd Aberteifi ..**19** B5
Ysgol y Bedol **22** F5
Ysgol y Ddwerwen **11** D2
Ysgol y Drefach **28** G3
Ysgol y Glyn **27** A6
Ysgol y Ddwylan **31** A2

INDUSTRIAL ESTATES

Amex Park **11** C5
Beechwood Ind. Estate **29** C1
Betws Industrial Park **10** F3
Betws Park Bus. Centre **10** E4
Bridge Meadow Retail Estate
....**13** D4
Brook Trading Estate **13** A6
Capel Hendre Ind. Estate ..**25** B6
Church Bank Ind. Estate......**29** A6
Church Road Ind. Estate **20** E3
Cillefwr Industrial Estate **11** A5
Cleddau Business Park **18** G1
Cross Hands Bus. Park **20** G4
Emlyn Industrial Estate........**31** C2
Feidr Castell Bus. Park........**21** D4
Fenton Industrial Estate **14** E3
Glanaman Workshops **22** F2
Glanyrafon Industrial Estate ..**8** G3
Goodwick Industrial Estate ..**21** A2
Havens Head Bus. Park **15** D4
Havens Head Retail Park **15** D4
Haverfordwest Business Centre*,
Winch Lane **14** E4
Honeyborough Ind. Estate ..**32** F4
Kingswood Trading Estate ..**18** H4
Llanbadarn Industrial Estate ..**8** F4
Llanbed Industrial Estate **28** G4
Llannion Park Ind. Estate **18** F2
London Road Ind. Estate **18** H3
Maritime Industrial Estate ...**18** E2
Myrtle Hill Retail Area **11** C5
Narbeth Bridge Bus. Estate **30** F4
Newport Business Park **31** C5
Old School Ind. Estate **30** G5
Parc Amanwy Ind. Estate **9** D5
Parc Hendre Ind. Estate **25** C6
Parc Pensarn Retail Area **12** E5
Parc Teifi Business Park **19** C5
Parc y Llyn Retail Park **7** D4
Pentood Industrial Estate ...**19** D5
Raven Industrial Estate **22** G5
Salterns Ind. Estate, The **26** F4
Spring Gardens Ind. Estate **35** D2
St. Clears Business Park **33** C2
Technium **7** B3
Teifi Valley Bus. Centre **31** C3
Thornton Business Park **16** F2
Thornton Industrial Estate...**16** F2
Waterloo Industrial Estate ..**18** G3
West Wales Business Park..**30** F4
Withybush Retail Estate **13** C5
Withybush Trading Estate ..**13** A5